The Extremely Busy Woman's Guide to Self-Care

ALSO BY SUZANNE FALTER

nonfiction

The Joy of Letting Go

Surrendering to Joy: My Year of Love, Letting Go, and Forgiveness

How Much Joy Can You Stand?: How to Push Past
   Your Fears and Create Your Dreams

fiction

Driven

Committed

Destined

coauthored with jack harvey

Transformed: San Francisco

Transformed: Paris

Transformed: POTUS

The Extremely Busy Woman's Guide to Self-Care

Do Less, Achieve More, and Live the Life You Want

SUZANNE FALTER

 sourcebooks

Published by Sourcebooks
P.O. Box 4410, Naperville, Illinois 60567-4410
(630) 961-3900
sourcebooks.com

Printed and bound in the United States of America.
VP 10 9 8 7 6 5 4 3 2 1

for the healers, friends, and fellows
who showed me the path to self-care

and for Teal

contents

part one: the self-care mindset   1

part two: self-care essentials   145

part three: working self-care
  into your life   249

your self-care log   290

acknowledgments   294
about the author   295

part one

the self-care mindset

one

why we all crave self-care

. . . .

Presumably, you picked up this book because the cover spoke to you. The idea of indulging in a lovely warm bath of ideas and encouragement about self-care appealed to you. Or maybe a friend recommended it—a friend with a little too much empathy in her eyes.

One way or another, you crave self-care because, on some level, it's missing in your life.

But if you're like some of us, that fact could be hard to admit. You may think you're one of the few people out there who doesn't actually need self-care. You may tell yourself you're just too busy for self-care. Or you offer up your annual massage and your occasional weekend off as proof that you're just fine.

Secretly, part of you may believe you're just a little superhuman and don't need the same stuff the rest of us do. And yet, here you are, reading this book.

You may insist that you'd get to self-care if only there weren't so many other people and projects out there demanding your attention. Or maybe you're a procrastinator. You really are going to start taking better care of yourself...soon!

Or it could be a major piece of your life has just fallen apart. You've been left mildly stunned, knowing something must change and feeling utterly overwhelmed at the prospect.

Maybe you just flat out know you need self-care, and you need help with it. Now!

Whatever the case may be, your future as a self-caring individual can begin this minute, but only if you are willing. The fact is that I know what you're going through, because not too long ago, I was you.

I was busy. Lord, I was busy! Meanwhile, I hid from my own needs for decades. When they occurred to me, I simply suppressed them. The voices around me drowned out my own, even when it came to my sexuality. In a telling example, I avoided the fact that I was a lesbian for thirty-three years because it would be so horribly inconvenient to my homophobic parents.

I also buried myself in work, which turned out to be a really good place to hide from my general state of dissatisfaction.

I simply didn't know that I mattered. I thought I was supposed to become a stressed-out, wired, unconscious doormat to the world. I thought I was supposed to work ever harder in some skewed attempt to become the most brilliant, the most perfect, the most *whatever*.

It wasn't until life finally stopped me in my tracks that I began to regroup. Only then did I learn how critical self-care is to a life well lived. And only then did I realize that this seemingly self-indulgent activity was actually the truest path back to happiness.

What happened was that my twenty-two-year-old daughter, Teal, suddenly died from a medically unexplainable cardiac arrest.

One minute, we were sitting in a café in San Francisco, enjoying a lovely dinner. Two hours later, she was in a coma. Six days later, she was dead. That was the moment I went from being a stressed-out, overworked, self-involved internet marketing consultant to being an incoherent lump on a bed.

As the months passed and I grieved Teal's death, I began to see everything I had been doing as meaningless. Slowly, over time, it dawned on me that I felt lost and empty because I didn't want this life I'd cobbled together

By this point in my life, I'd managed to embrace my lesbianism and leave my marriage, but that was about it. I was pursuing a career that was inauthentic, and my first lesbian relationship was an unmitigated disaster that had just ended.

Finally, I was being forced to tell the truth I'd run from for far too long. But once I admitted that I didn't actually want the relationship or the career, an even more frightening realization surfaced.

I had no idea what I *did* want.

Suitcase in hand, I left the home I'd shared with my former partner. I put my things in storage, packed up my car, and began to wander.

When you're used to being completely harried, uncertainty is downright scary. Twice in the year that followed, I tried to return to my former work, and twice, I fell flat on my face. My website got hacked repeatedly. A relaunch of a product that had once done well failed miserably. No matter how I tried to avoid the empty space, I couldn't. The universe kept telling me to go back to bed.

My only job was to relax, grieve, and not know what to do next. I had enough savings to live on for a year or two if I was very, very frugal, so I stopped. Completely.

In that big, long stretch of not working—and not doing much of anything, really, besides grieving—I discovered the cure to my aggravation, my sleeplessness, and my pain. In that quiet stillness, I began to listen to myself.

Slowly, I admitted the things that weren't working.

I took responsibility for the suffering I'd caused others. I forgave myself and everyone else as well. And I started trying on new activities, like consciously listening to people and keeping quiet for a change. And I learned to ask for help. Instead of second-guessing and doubting those around me, I began to actually trust them.

Gradually, a bit of light began to dawn. I became aware of things I cared about, like singing, something I hadn't even thought about for nearly a decade. And writing fiction, which I hadn't done in years.

Instead of being so wrapped up in work I didn't like and heroically solving everyone else's problems, I began thinking about myself with a new curiosity. What did I want from each day? What did I need?

This was how I discovered what self-care is really all about. For me, it wasn't scheduling yet another massage, a therapy appointment, or anything else. Instead, it became about *un-scheduling* my days. My new life was about nothing more than slowing down and going within.

Yes, I grieved. In fact, I grieved a great deal. But in that grief and introspection, I also reinvented my life.

If my daughter was going to die and I was going to live, I simply couldn't go on the way I had been. The only way back to peace and serenity was to become a better person, the kind of person who listened to herself attentively and actively lived her values.

I wanted to be someone Teal would have been proud of.

In fact, as I moved through my grief, I began to read the journals Teal had left behind. In particular, I devoured a worn, red spiral notebook filled with insights and short bits of reassurance she'd written out. What became extraordinarily clear was how dedicated to self-care she had been in her own life.

Teal had epilepsy, which left her extremely attuned to her body. She was always listening and responding accordingly. Yet her approach to self-care was far more than that.

Unlike many people, Teal was excellent at simply being. She had few ambitions in life beyond the next spontaneous trip to some far-flung corner of the world with her backpack and her guitar in hand. All she knew was that ultimately, someday, she wanted to be a healer.

Teal delighted in the simple joy of connecting with other people, both strangers and friends. She enjoyed the grace of resting as needed, and she never pushed herself. Furthermore, Teal had little use for material wealth and the stuff the rest of us surround ourselves with.

When she died, she had two dollars in her wallet and another five in her bank account. Yet only days before, when I asked if she needed any money, she told me she didn't. She had enough, she said. After all, she had just bought groceries.

What Teal understood—and I was just learning—was that life was inherently rich just as it is, without a lot of bells and whistles added.

In the days that passed, I learned that self-care is ultimately about the exquisite act of simply being, without needing to be useful, effective, organized, ambitious, or even good.

It is about stopping the endless doing and letting life flow around us, carrying us, as we begin to pay close attention to our wants and needs.

Within that state of being, my life slowly began to bloom again. Two years after Teal's death, when I was finally, truly ready and not one moment sooner, new work suddenly arrived. An investor called me up out of the blue and offered to fund a series of novels that I would write, even though I hadn't published fiction for twenty-four years.

It was writing I wanted to do, so I said yes. Not long after that, I happened to go to a party where I met the love of my life. We married two years later. Along the way, I was invited to sing with an R & B band after meeting some of the players at a spontaneous music jam. Yet another bucket list item was surprisingly ticked off.

Then, remarkably, my career as a speaker was rekindled through a series of events that began when we donated Teal's organs after her death. One kidney and her liver went to women in their fifties and sixties. Her heart and her other kidney went to a young woman, not much older than Teal, who'd struggled with congestive heart failure for eight years. The sense that there was a purpose to Teal's inexplicable death became hugely reassuring to me.

One day, I was chatting with the donor network outreach

coordinator. During the previous year, she'd dutifully checked in from time to time, making sure I had everything I needed as I grieved. And at that time, I was at a turning point in my grief as I moved back toward day-to-day functioning.

"Do you happen to be a speaker?" she asked me toward the end of our conversation. In fact, I'd spoken extensively in my writing and consulting careers and created and led hundreds of workshops.

"I am," I replied. "How did you know?"

The coordinator paused. "I have no idea," she admitted.

Then she went on to explain that few donor families were willing to speak about their experiences on stage. If I was, it would help their audiences of transplant professionals, for whom burnout was always a risk. All of them needed to be reminded from time to time about the value of their intensely stressful work.

Soon, I found myself delivering keynote speeches and workshops to audiences of hundreds of health care and organ transplantation workers around the United States.

Again and again, I shared my experience as a donor mom from the stage. I also told the story of how Teal's death led me to discover the value of self-care. I shared precious little nuggets from her journals every time.

It was work I never would have expected to do in a million years.

As I spread this message, I also wrote hundreds of blog posts, some of which went viral on Facebook. My essays were then picked up by major magazines and online journals, and I began the *Self-Care for Extremely Busy Women* podcast. An online course and the Self-Care Group for Extremely Busy Women on Facebook followed.

Day by day, I discovered that harried women everywhere were struggling with self-care just as I once had. And I realized that together, Teal and I could provide a solution.

So she got to live out her dream of being a healer, albeit posthumously. And I found my way back to my true purpose—one that truly honors who I am.

How did any of this happen? For once, I stopped. I let go and took good care of myself, and the deeply aligned life I'd craved for so long just arrived and settled in.

The only "work" I had to do was to take responsibility for my path, tell the truth, and begin to listen to myself closely. And to say yes when opportunities arose.

This, I've come to learn, is the true path of self-care. It is a way of effortlessness in which much gets done but without all the drama, the struggle, or the overwork.

Instead, it is a path of grace that guides you impeccably, but only when you are ready and willing to examine your own life.

Bear in mind that you don't have to have a crisis to get the point. You just have to crave and welcome the self-care that will deliver you to the life of your dreams.

True self-care is about honoring your heart and soul. And I am here to say this is exactly what you deserve, whoever you are and whatever you have done until now. To paraphrase Mary Oliver's glorious poem "Wild Geese," you really don't have to walk through the desert on your knees for mile after mile to be worthy.

You just have to be willing to get up, dust yourself off, and begin again.

two

why this is not a book about time management

. . . .

I used to think all my problems could be solved with more time. I imagined an extra weekend ought to do it.

If I could only find the space to breathe, my difficult relationship, my hectic career, and the strange, lonely emptiness I kept experiencing would finally settle down. Then I'd be happy again, I told myself. Finally, I'd be able to relax.

Or so I thought.

True deep, delicious self-care isn't about time management, taking the weekend off, or getting a regular massage, though those things can certainly help. Nor is it about working to the point of exhaustion and then retreating to a spa for an afternoon. Or using meditation, chardonnay, and TV binges to zone out after yet another toxic fight with your loved one.

It's about creating a better life overall, one that's aligned with your values and who you actually are.

It's about honoring the still, small voice within that guides you, impeccably, to become your best self. And it's about having the courage to make changes that truly reflect you and what your beautiful, sensitive, beating heart desires more than anything.

To do this, you begin by tuning in to yourself and listening to your body, and this can be hard at first. You may observe your dreams and write them down. Perhaps you journal as well. Maybe when you tune in, you hear nothing at first. Or maybe you just notice sudden thoughts while you're taking a shower.

One way or another, once you commit to the path of self-care and you begin to listen in earnest, a pronounced trail of bread crumbs shows up as life reveals what's *really* next for you. You may know what I'm talking about because your body and soul are already talking to you—quite loudly, even.

They may, in fact, be telling you to slow down. And that thought can be downright scary. Yet here is the truth about our life in the twenty-first century:

Most of us do far more than we need to.

We live in a culture that favors doing over being and intensity over serenity. We are taught to overproduce at an early age, ever stepping up our games to become higher and higher achievers who learn how to compete, push, and drive ourselves into the ground.

And yet, what if all that overproduction was actually unnecessary? What if we just showed up and did a good-enough, adequate job instead of one that is mind-blowingly superb?

What if we earned *enough* money and had *enough* stuff instead of needing to rake in ever more dough and drive an ever-spiffier car?

Would that actually be enough for us? Could we live with ourselves if we didn't live up to the hype that resonates through our culture?

Could we settle for "perfectly fine" instead of "extraordinary"?

If this concept seems foreign or downright wrong, consider this. You and I have little perspective about our lives. Or at least we don't until the bottom drops out and everything falls apart. Then the view is glaringly clear.

You may read this and think I'm down on human achievement. Hey, I love achievement! Without it, we wouldn't be where we are today. And yet, a steady diet of overachievement leaves us with broken bodies and stressful, empty lives that are devoid of meaning.

I'm suggesting there is a time and place for each of us to stop and reflect on what we're doing with these beautiful lives we've been given. And then to make changes where necessary.

Only when you take a clear, unflinching look at your life and really see exactly where you're at can you begin to take better care of yourself. And that's when life gets really good.

What's on the other side of all that personal discovery and self-care is true, unequivocal happiness. That much I can promise you. You may have to make a few changes first or at least develop a few new habits. That can mean stepping out of your comfort zone for a while.

But trust me on this. You are really, *really* going to like where you wind up, because it will be the most deliciously free, authentic, in-flow place you can imagine. This is what happens when you listen to your inner longings.

Now, you could be reading this thinking none of this applies to you. You know you are just too damn busy to ever consider taking time off. But I'm not advocating that you do. I'm simply advocating for a pause to reflect.

And I'm providing another perspective on how to get underneath your current state of busyness so you can dig into what you need and even actively crave in your life.

It could be that this book triggers some new ideas for you about how to manage your busyness. Or it encourages you to ask for support you never realized you needed. Or it opens your mind to adding some new creative meanderings to your day.

Whatever it does for you, may it free that inner spirit who longs to speak to you. And may it empower you to listen to her well.

How to Maximize Your Use of This Book

Here's what I know about women like us. We like to get things done. That means a lot of us have no interest in little fussy questionnaires or exercises that pop up right in the middle of a good read.

But we also like results.

Do yourself a favor, and actually take a few moments to complete the various exercises, lists, and questionnaires that follow. I've kept them as brief (and as fun) as possible. Hey, I've even timed them for you! Think of them as your ticket to much improved self-care, for they will help you tell yourself the all-critical truth.

If you're reading electronically, bring a notebook or a blank document to make notes in as you go along.

In part 1, you'll find ideas and exercises about the inner work of self-care. In part 2, you'll discover tips on how to make these healthier habits part of every day.

Be someone in the world
who loves loving yourself!

—TEAL'S JOURNAL, AUGUST 17, 2011

three
how stressed out are you?

It's like there's something in the water.

According to the American Psychological Association, 75 percent of all respondents to a recent survey on stress said they'd experienced at least one symptom of acute stress in the previous month.*

This means three out of four Americans currently experience stress.

To get a pulse on exactly how stressed you are and how much you may need greater self-care, please fill out the following checklist. Check off any symptoms you've had in the last three months.

----

*   Christopher Bergland, "Stress in America Is Gnawing Away at Our Well-Being," *Psychology Today*, November 1, 2017, https://www.psychologytoday.com/us/blog/the -athletes-way/201711/stress-in-america-is-gnawing-away-our-overall-well-being.

Common Symptoms of Stress

☐ Headache

☐ Body and muscle aches or muscle tension

☐ Acne or pimples

☐ Chest pain and rapid heartbeat

☐ Fatigue or low energy

☐ Change in sex drive, ability

☐ Stomach upset, diarrhea, constipation

☐ Butterflies in the stomach

☐ Frequent heartburn

☐ Sleep issues

☐ Anxiety

☐ Restlessness

☐ Lack of focus

☐ Lack of motivation

☐ Feeling overwhelmed

☐ Becoming easily frustrated, moodiness

☐ Irritability or anger

☐ Sadness and depression

☐ Undereating

☐ Overeating

☐ Angry outbursts

☐ Substance abuse

☐ Tobacco use

☐ Social withdrawal

☐ Exercising less often

☐ Inability to relax

☐ Low self-esteem

☐ Loneliness

☐ Avoiding others

☐ Frequent colds and infections

☐ Nervousness, shaking

☐ Ringing in the ears

☐ Cold or sweaty hands and feet

☐ Excess sweating

☐ Dry mouth, difficulty swallowing

☐ Clenched jaw and teeth grinding

☐ Hair loss

☐ Shakiness and weakness due to low blood sugar

☐ Feeling faint or fainting

☐ Poor judgment

☐ Developing nervous habits such as nail biting, twitching

☐ Weight fluctuations

What to Do with Your Results

Ask yourself right now how the stress symptoms you just checked off stack up to, say, a year ago? Five years ago?

Are there a number of new ones? Or have you been nursing the same old stress symptoms for a long time?

Have you been avoiding your stress or pretending it's not there? Or have you been working on it but not making much progress so far?

The important thing is not to resolve the stress in this moment but to see it for what it is. Simply observe it for now. Then keep reading and doing the exercises.

There are ideas ahead that will be of help.

four

the big illusion about getting stuff done

. . . .

When I was younger, I used to think that my all-important goals in life could only be achieved one way: by doing stuff.

The very idea of relaxing and taking a day off seemed like anathema to me. If I wasn't working, working, working, I was hitting the treadmill to improve my blood-oxygen level. Or I was meditating so I could make my neural connectivity zoom. Or perhaps I was reading lots of books on how to become ever more productive and successful.

I even treated motherhood like an exercise in overachievement, painstakingly making chicken croquettes to hide scary green vegetables and researching which baby board books provided the maximum infant brain stimulation.

Back then, I worked my heart out because secretly, I believed I was flawed. I thought I had to try harder than everyone else to compensate for what was a basic loser package.

For years, I kept up a nonstop quest to become Super Susie. It was exhausting. At one point, a friend noticed this and asked me, "When do you ever relax?"

"I do yoga twice a week!" I shot back, and my friend shook her head.

Clearly, I'd missed the point.

What I didn't yet realize is that those goals of mine could have been more easily reached if I'd just stopped. By busying up my life, I'd taken away one of the most critical components of self-care, which is rest.

Space.

Plain old emptiness.

Back then, I didn't yet see that I was, in fact, mortal and that I needed to restore myself periodically. And I really didn't see the connection between my general success level and my self-care. At least I didn't until I met a friend I'll call Marianne.

Marianne, like me, was an online entrepreneur whose income relied on lots of content creation, marketing, and networking. Yet unlike me, Marianne made self-care her biggest priority every single day.

I know this because Marianne and I were "action buddies." We'd email each other a list of to-dos in our lives and our businesses. Then we'd check in later in the day with a report of how we'd done. My list usually had seventeen items stuffed into an eight- or ten-hour work period.

Marianne's list had four, three of which were items like "Hike Pinesaw Ridge," "Get a manicure," and "Sign up for a cleanse."

I wondered about this but decided Marianne must be a business lightweight. Then I actually had lunch with her one day, and she shared the details of her business. Marianne was, in fact, making a healthy six-figure salary, which was a whole lot more than me.

"Oh, I work hard sometimes," she said airily. "But I've learned that taking care of myself usually helps me make more money."

Huh?

That set me back on my heels. It took a long time for this new reality to sink in, but eventually, it did. What Marianne shared with me was the critical importance of putting yourself first and simply trusting yourself to achieve your dreams without having to run yourself into the ground.

Marianne demonstrated to me that I was worth investing in first. Once I did so, my body got recharged and ready to go, and my instincts became sharper and more nuanced. Both things were inherently useful as I moved forward, not as a superachiever but actually just as plain old, fired-up and excited me.

Slowly, tentatively, I began to experiment with this new reality. I folded it in with everything else I was learning as I redid my life.

As I began my new work as a novelist, I made a conscious decision that I was never going to overwork again. I wasn't going to sneak work in on the weekends or late at night as I had done in my previous life. And I wasn't going to grind myself to dust by the end of each day in yet another failed attempt to be "enough."

Instead, I was going to decide I already was enough. And I would work no more than five or six hours on any given workday. Then the *entire rest of each day would be used for self-care*.

For me, a life well lived was no longer about working harder. Instead, it was about working smarter. This seemed radical, but it also seemed right. All I knew was that I couldn't go back to my old way of doing things.

As I got back to work, what happened was amazing. I noticed I wanted to add lots and lots of work tasks to my day, just as I had before. But I also noticed that my perspective had shifted.

Now I could add those items...or not. I could blow off the extra stuff if I wanted to and not even feel guilty about it. Suddenly, it was okay not to overachieve. And it was okay to ask for and receive a lot more help.

It was okay to just be normal.

I was enough, and my work was enough. This was amazingly freeing.

I turned to my self-care time with gusto. I began to swim in a lovely public pool on sunny afternoons. I went to a very relaxing yoga class when I wanted to. I lay in bed late into the mornings and noodled in my journal or simply drank tea and looked at the pond outside my window. And sometimes, when I needed to, I let myself grieve for my daughter. My work flowed in and around my self-care activities because I set my day up that way.

Actually booking that R & R time zone into my calendar was critical to being able to enjoy myself, guilt-free. Then, when I sat down to write, the words streamed in beautifully. The plots to the novels I wrote showed up without any struggle or suffering. I began to realize that my work life now existed entirely in a state of flow.

Over time, as my grief began to finally fade away, I added more work tasks. But I also made a point of adding in equal time for visiting with friends and for simply having some fun. I started cooking more elaborate meals and planned some dinner parties with my housemate. I joined a choir. Then the R & B band found me.

Several years later, I'm still living pretty much the same way, and I have no plans to change. Each day, I wake up, listen to my body, and set up the day in accordance with what I want and need. And every afternoon, my self-care zone begins at three or four in the afternoon, come hell or high water. The key difference is that now I produce far more work. (More on this interesting phenomenon later.)

Somehow, the tasks get done, if not today, then tomorrow. I've gotten a lot better at prioritizing what actually has to happen, what can be delegated, and what can simply wait. When you tell the truth about it, everything does *not* have to happen right now. That's just the crying of a frazzled mind, particularly if you're inclined to overachieve.

I write this after having a lovely cup of tea with my friend Kenji, a break I never would have taken in the old days. And what's the result? Now I can relax as I do my work, feeling strong and centered in my core...and wonderfully at peace.

So, you ask, how does this relate to you, a person with a fixed schedule who has to show up in a workplace every day? That's what we'll be examining in the rest of this book.

The fact is that every decision you make about how you spend your days and how you treat yourself can, indeed, be rethought.

This is your invitation to stretch out, relax, and reconsider how you roll.

May you enjoy the ride.

Finished meditating and got such a strong message... Stay where you are and all will be the same.

—TEAL'S JOURNAL, AUGUST 17, 2011

five

a portrait of your typical day

Write down a list of people, places, and things that are currently part of your typical days, both at home and at work.

Allow yourself to conjure up the whole picture—the assistant you get annoyed with, the office flirt who makes you cringe, the hellish traffic. Feel free to add the lovely moments as well, like commuting with a great podcast in your ears, sweet moments with your children, or a rapturous early morning walk.

As you summon up each picture, do not filter anything out. Instead, let your mind produce a complete picture of your current reality and get it all down. Tell the entire, unvarnished truth. *Do not edit.* Just write.

My Typical Day at Home

My Typical Day at Work

six

does your self-care truly support you?

Please answer the following questions as honestly as possible. This is the best way to find out how you are doing and what you need.

The best phrase I could use right now to describe myself is

a. On fire!

b. Content

c. Clouded and somewhat distracted

d. Downright cranky or depressed

e. Stressed out and completely overwhelmed

I would describe my energy in general as

a. Abundant

b. Pretty good

c. Seeking a new level but not there yet

   d. Harried

   e. Just plain exhausted

When I think about my current level of self-care, I feel

   a. Happy and proud of myself

   b. A little worried

   c. I know it's wrong, but I can't stop and change it

   d. I don't like to think about it

   e. Sad and frustrated, maybe even angry

My health is

   a. Excellent

   b. A work in progress

   c. Currently neglected, but I'll get to it...maybe

   d. A problem I know I need to solve but I don't know how

   e. Chronically or seriously poor or imbalanced

The way I use my time is

   a. Perfect, feels really in flow

   b. Okay but could be better

   c. There is too much to do

   d. Obviously in need of repair

   e. Feeling completely overwhelmed and suffocated

The way I manage my work is

    a.   In harmony with my heart and soul

    b.   Getting to some point of balance

    c.   A disorganized jumble

    d.   Can't stop working...it will never all get done!

    e.   Serious overwork or work-avoidant

My relationship to exercise is

    a.   Fun, an important part of my life

    b.   Can't stick to a regular exercise program but I try

    c.   I keep meaning to get to this, and occasionally I do

    d.   I go for long periods without exercise

    e.   Nonexistent

When it comes to friends and community, I know

    a.   I am loved and have plenty

    b.   I have a few friends I connect with, but I could use more

    c.   I don't have time for this too

    d.   I attract friends who drain my energy or use me

    e.   I don't have any or have lost touch with them

When it comes to love, I am

    a.   Really satisfied and happy

    b.   Longing for more of something

    c.   Currently in a breakup or recovering from one

    d.   Can't seem to stop attracting the wrong kind of person

    e.   Feeling lost and alone

I would describe my finances as

   a.   Solid and predictable in a good way

   b.   Getting under control and feeling better as I go

   c.   I binge with spending and debt, or I live in some deprivation

   d.   Money is uncertain and scary to me

   e.   Financially overwhelmed; it's one of my biggest issues in life

When it comes to taking a vacation just to feed my soul, I typically

   a.   Do it on a regular basis, and I benefit every time

   b.   Do so occasionally and know I need more

   c.   Know I need one, but I'm not sure how to make it happen

   d.   Figure I can't spend that much time on myself

   e.   Avoid it; it seems impossible

When I think about the support in my life, I feel

   a.   Amply supported and highly grateful

   b.   Okay overall with a few gaps

   c.   I could use more but am not sure where to find it

   d.   I don't need support; I can do it myself

   e.   Completely overwhelmed and don't know where to turn

Assess Your Responses

Take a look at how you answered the preceding questions. You may need far more self-care than you currently give yourself, or you may be right on track. Either way, use this exercise to learn more about what could be next for you.

Here is a quick, rough guide you can use to score the quiz.

▶ **Mostly a's:** You are in a place of abundant self-care. Congratulations! What can you do to make sure you keep up with your good habits?

▶ **Mostly b's:** What kind of self-care best supports this great expansion you are in right now?

▶ **Mostly c's:** It is easy to be overwhelmed by life, isn't it? But you know there is work to do in your self-care. Has the time finally come?

▶ **Mostly d's:** It's hard to give yourself permission to stop and reflect, and there is a lot to reflect on here. Can you give yourself permission to rest for a while?

▶ **Mostly e's:** Sometimes we get to a point in life where all we can do is fall apart. But on the other side of that falling apart is pure gold. The trick is to fall apart in a way that is really supported, with the help of a therapist, support groups, or the loving care of people who understand you. Most importantly, you have the opportunity right now to grow—and to come back to yourself. This book can be a helpful beginning, so read on!

Reminder:
Unless you take care of
yourself first,
you cannot take care
of anyone else.

seven
have you forgotten who you are?

....

When you were little, you had a vibrant spark. Its flame lit you up, filled you with ideas, and generally made you content. Perhaps you still have that spark.

On the other hand, it might have gone out a while ago.

You'll know because when you wake up in the morning, there's either a leap-out-of-bed-and-hit-the-ground-running feeling, or there's a subtle dread. The vibrant spark would correspond to the former. And it's the key to your contentment.

If you read this and think you're too old for the vibrant spark, au contraire, dear reader. I refer you to my former neighbor Dorothy, whom I encountered one morning at seven a.m. when she was *returning* from a morning wildlife trek in the woods in a foot of snow…at age eighty-three. In fifteen-degree Fahrenheit weather.

"Lovely to be up with the sun, isn't it?" she asked with a smile.

When we feel that precious spark, we're simply glad to be alive. Things are working in our lives, and we're humming along, eager to get to the next thing.

This is, in fact, how we are hooked up from birth. We're hardwired for happiness. Yet so often, our fear has pulled us away from the natural path of our desires, our interests, and our personal quirks.

I'm here to advocate for that essential return to you-ness. It's a very big piece of excellent self-care. In fact, it's the most essential part.

So here are a few questions to get you going on the highway back to you.

You are stressed. You just need to have a good cry and let it all go.

—TEAL'S JOURNAL, OCTOBER 15, 2011

····· TWENTY MINUTES ·····

Remembering Who You Are

What are some activities or places you adored when you were a little kid?

Who did you hope you'd become when you grew up?

What are three of your happiest memories?

What have you been longing to do?

Whom have you been longing to see?

Where have you been longing to go?

What are some things you still deeply enjoy?

What's missing in your life that needs to be retrieved?

eight
the five basics
of self-care

....

What does it actually take to live a life that's rich with self-care? There are five basic elements.

1. Understand your needs.

You've got them, just like we all do. Sometimes the signals scream at you, like when you suddenly wake up with a seriously tweaked lower back. Pretty tough to ignore, right?

While you're pumping the ibuprofen, consider this. Your aching back may be trying to tell you something about some aspect of your life where your needs are getting ignored. Especially if you had no precipitating fall, twist, strain, or intense new exercise that could have taxed you.

Chances are this pain has nothing to do with your back per se but instead is using that part of your body as a very loud megaphone. The same is often true for all sorts of chronic, stress-related illnesses like eczema, insomnia, gut issues, heart disease, fibromyalgia, and even herpes. When these kinds of conditions flare up, it's a great time to stop, quiet down, and ask yourself—or even your aching body part—what you need.

See what answer swims up first. Then, instead of fleeing, over-writing, or ignoring it, just take note.

On the other hand, your needs might express themselves much more quietly. For instance, you keep meaning to call your dear old Aunt Sally, but who has the time? Still, Aunt Sally lingers in the back of your mind, and the thought chides you on a regular basis. One night in the middle of the night, you wake up knowing you really do need to talk to Aunt Sally. Like *now*.

This is the kind of need that, when you're extremely busy, is easy to ignore. After all, you've barely spent any time in the last several years with Aunt Sally, even though you adored her when you were a child. You decide Aunt Sally can get along for one more day without hearing from you, and you carry on as if nothing had happened.

But then comes that terrible moment when you find out that Aunt Sally suddenly died. You didn't speak to her, you feel guilty and ashamed of yourself, and so it goes.

Another unmet need becomes one more arrow in the quiver of self-inflicted arrows that ultimately take you down.

It's remarkably hard when you are very busy to allow yourself to follow that tenuous path back to your heart. So often, those moments just seem so unimportant, and honoring them may feel completely counterintuitive and like genuine time wasters.

Yet here's where the magic is.

The unexplainable desire to connect with Aunt Sally was a message from none other than your heart and soul, the very same part of you that keeps getting ignored as you press ever forward with your to-do list. By stopping and actually listening to that critical voice within and acting on it, you give yourself a small, precious gift.

As you begin to meet your needs, life suddenly shifts and becomes remarkably easier. You find you can breathe again. The more you do this, the more your life begins to change.

This is when the drama stops. People around you seem to become more respectful and loving, and the out-and-out assholes disappear. Meanwhile, you become kinder and more relaxed. As you begin to tune into yourself more and more and honor those seemingly innocuous instincts, your life simply improves.

This is how you learn to do less, achieve more, and live in peace. By simply understanding and honoring your needs.

2. Set boundaries.

It's remarkable how hard it is for some of us to say no, right?

It may feel like someone's always nipping at our heels, trying to get in there with a request. There may be a virtual avalanche of requests coming at us all the time. Or so it seems if we've been in the habit of saying yes all the time. Because once those boundaries get trampled, the rest of the world comes barreling in.

You may find yourself agreeing to things you don't want to do but then muttering to yourself, "I'll just get through this, and then everything will be okay," or "Just this one last time." That, my friend, is a red flag.

How do you know where you and your boundaries begin and end? It's all about your agitation level.

Notice how your body reacts when a request is made. If you're like some of us, your mind will say yes while your body is screaming "NO! NO! NO!" That would be a significant boundary worth paying attention to.

Yet you may ignore your body. Instead, once again, the ever-compliant you says yes.

Of course, you have perfectly sensible reasons why. You tell yourself that somebody has to do it. Or that if you do the task, at least it will be done correctly. Or you convince yourself there's no one else who can do it or that there will be some sort of advantage down the road to agreeing.

And yet, your body did issue a firm, unequivocal no, didn't she? That was the voice of your soul, the living breathing heart of you that always looks out for your well-being. And when she says an unequivocal no, she means it. In other words, somewhere along the line, you will pay for this errant yes.

The beautiful thing about boundaries is that your body always tells you just where they are, even if you don't always agree.

Meanwhile, your good excuses become very flimsy when held up to the light of reason. For instance, there are definitely other people who can do this unwanted task instead of you. If you died tomorrow, it would still presumably get done, wouldn't it? And if not, maybe it wasn't that important to begin with. And as for getting the job done "right," consider this. There may be someone you don't even know who might do this job better than you.

In the end, no one knows where your boundaries begin and end but you. The question is whether you will honor them.

3. Ask for help as needed.

Some of us are a lot better at this than others. But for the most part, we're a steely, independent lot, us hardworking women. We don't want no help, no how.

And yet, think about how much easier that might actually be. Then you might get a little time to breathe and think and simply be. Then life might calm down significantly if you could just delegate or even find someone to lean on.

Still, if you're like many of us, you convince yourself that you don't need any help. "By the time I explain all this to someone else, I could have done it myself twice," you say. Or you insist you have enough help, even though you're a frantic mess by day's end.

Consider this. What if you reject getting adequate help because it might make you feel vulnerable?

Would accepting help somehow make you feel less heroic and more...sigh...human? Allowing in help may simply mean that you are not the rock star you think you are. And if so, well, you're not alone.

When you actually allow in support, then you have some extra time on your hands. Which means you can then get in touch with all those feelings you've been avoiding.

All it takes is one quiet evening, you know.

If it sounds like I'm trying to get you to rethink how you've been rolling, it's true.

I am.

4. Take action.

Before you get excited about this one, let me be clear.

I'm not talking about "working hard" at self-care or even sneaking in items from your lengthy to-do list. Instead, I'm saying take steps that undo your old, steely habits of self-neglect. Even if that step is to do nothing and relax.

Take action by reading this book and doing the exercises. Take action by being courageous enough to do things differently, to get out of your comfort zone and ask for help. Listen to your body, and do what it asks you to do.

Take action even by taking a rest.

It may feel strange, but I promise it's okay.

5. Build self-care into your day.

Once you've begun to get in touch with what you want and need and you've adjusted your boundaries and learned to ask for help, there's one final critical step. Take those new, mildly uncomfortable self-care habits you've discovered, and build them into your day.

I'm talking about automation here. You pay bills like your car insurance automatically, right? So why not set up a schedule that automatically builds in meditation, exercise, massages, and time to just sit around and relax?

Why not get the help you need—one way or another—to make this happen? Because if you don't set up actual habits and systems to support this new life you're building, delicious self-care items like getaways, naps, and journaling time quickly get ignored.

If you're serious about destressing and enjoying more self-care, then your schedule must begin with you and your needs. After that, you can begin to fold in the rest of the world, in moderation, where possible. And only if it soothes your soul.

Really.

You can do it.

nine
why you may resist self-care

. . . .

Have you ever noticed that we are fatally flawed?

Our psyches understand and know the incredible power of self-care to put life back in balance, and yet, we fight it. We procrastinate, avoid, cancel, deny, and even break appointments with massage therapists at the last minute. Call it a design glitch in the human psyche.

"I'm just too busy!" we cry. And that's where we get stuck.

We *are* too busy, which, of course, is the problem. Schedules become dangerous weapons in our hands as we compulsively say yes to more and more. Self-care falls off the schedule, or it gets firmly delegated to the last spot on our to-do lists. (And, of course, we never get to it.)

There are four basic reasons we avoid self-care. First, somewhere back in the subterranean reaches of our minds, we may think we don't deserve it. Long ago, we made a decision that everyone else should come first.

You know this is you if, say, your mother can railroad you into agreeing to come over and pick paint colors instead of going to your support group meeting. Or your boss can get you to stay late on yet another Friday night, even if it also happens to be your wedding anniversary. Or you find yourself volunteering for yet another good cause, even though you promised yourself you'd stop saying yes.

You know this is you because back there somewhere may also be a spouse, some kids, and even a friend shaking their head and wondering how they can get you to stop.

Or perhaps you feel on some basic level you haven't given yourself permission for self-care. Somehow, it's not in your personal schema for life. Other people who do make copious time for self-care may even seem mildly suspicious.

Though we hate to admit it, some of us may also take a certain delight in the suffering that comes with self-deprivation. There may be a certain nobility about not having our needs met. Perhaps we even complain about this loudly in hopes of gaining sympathy and admiration.

In the end, it's all about what you tell yourself.

Perhaps you don't want to take on the feelings that come with slowing down and stopping. Frenetic activity is a great place to hide from the realities of life, realities like grief, loneliness, and even fear. If that's you, you are not alone. I personally worked this angle for years. If I kept busy enough, focusing on my work and our kids, I didn't have to acknowledge, say, the problems with my marriage.

Most of us find we have to do something to keep such unpleasant realities out of our psyches, which could be why more than

70 percent of all Americans are obese or overweight.* Sometimes a piece of cheesecake is, well…medicinal.

Life is hard. Incredibly hard. That is a given fact. But rather than accept it and try to work with it, many of us get busy with subterfuge. We figure if we work hard enough, we can successfully avoid the parts of our life that are just not working.

And yet, you really can't hide, for sooner or later, your house of cards will fall apart. That much you can count on. The good news is that you have a choice about whether you'll let it get to that point. And fortunately, help is always at hand.

Still, many of us can't bring ourselves to stop and ask for help. We don't want it, we don't need it, and we will definitely resent it if you bring it up. Because although we may crave support, we still think we are somehow weak if we need help.

We figure we have to do all this alone. We tell ourselves the current reality is not so bad, and we reassure ourselves that we can do it. Then we forge on determinedly by ourselves.

For some of us, we are selective with the help we let in. Our souls may be dying under our mountainous workload, but some of us do have support staff. So that must mean we don't have a problem asking for help, right?

Not so fast.

It could be that your support staff is already stretched incredibly thin, but you can't bring yourself to do the asking and wrangling for

----

*   Centers for Disease Control, National Center for Health Statistics, https://www.cdc.gov/nchs/fastats/obesity-overweight.htm.

budget that more staff requires. Instead, you shoulder the burden and tell yourself to woman up.

Or it could be you can't bear to ask for the help you actually need, which is not around the office but within the reaches of your heart. If you reflexively flinch at the idea of therapy or life coaching, and if you'd rather die than spend the weekend doing a personal growth workshop, this could be you.

The remarkable thing is that no matter how you avoid it, your body will keep on craving self-care. It won't ever stop reminding you, whether this be by brute force or with a gentle whisper. Your body knows what it needs, and that would be balance.

Without balance in all things, you simply can't live the easeful, abundant life that you were given at birth. Instead, you will suffer. You will struggle and fall. You'll get up again and stagger on for a while, but you will keep failing in your ability to live a fully actualized life.

Something will always be missing, for when self-care and the resulting balance are not part of your life plan, your senses are not fully engaged. Your gifts become dulled, and as more and more distractions pile on, your brain gets somewhat disengaged.

And then, well, what's the point?

The invitation here is to look within.

Your judgment doesn't always follow your heart. Listen to your heart's desire.

—TEAL'S JOURNAL, AUGUST 2011

····· FIVE MINUTES ·····

What Holds You Back from Greater Self-Care?

Set a timer and write for five minutes on this question. Do not stop writing, even if you just keep scribbling, "I hate this stupid exercise." You may be surprised by what emerges.

Once you've finished, notice how you feel. Are you relieved? Moved? Anxious? Even actively afraid? Don't worry, because this is all part of the process. You are getting in touch with your own precious, wise emotions, and as ever, they will steer you well. Just keep allowing them to show up as you go through this book and move beyond. Great work!

ten

why we don't always know what we need

. . . .

When we avoid self-care, it's usually because we aren't paying particular attention to ourselves. Instead, we are focused on everyone else. And hey, they have a *lot* of needs.

You'll know this is you if you draw a blank when someone asks you what you need. The first time I became aware of this was just as my life began falling apart. A life coach put the question to me, and I have to say, I was dumbstruck.

I just...didn't know. It was as if my critical faculty had simply up and left. I sat there silently, groping around for an answer. What on earth *did* I need?

After a moment of awkward silence, I announced I needed some sleep, but did I really? Or was I just trying to come up with the first need I could think of?

Then I decided I must need a vacation as well, because it

had been months, if not years, since I'd taken one. I couldn't really remember my last true vacation when I didn't drag work along with me.

Then tears sprang into my eyes, and I saw in one horrifying moment just how much I needed that vacation. I'd denied myself one simply because years earlier, vacations had been financially difficult to take. Now, it was actually far easier. Yet I was still stuck in that tired old loop of impossibility.

After I realized that this was the twenty-first century and I actually could take a vacation—and even some naps—my whole body gave an unequivocal yes!

Once you begin tapping into those oh-so-buried needs, they will tumble forth, but it may take some digging to get there. Over time, as you get practiced at asking yourself what you need, your desires will flow forth more and more freely, especially if you listen to them and respond to them.

As for *why* these needs get buried in the first place, it's the same as with everything else. We are taught as children what we can and cannot have. And if we are raised by parents with problems of their own, our childhood needs may have taken a back seat to theirs.

This is especially true if one or both of your parents was an addict or had a personality disorder. Or it could be true if you had to take care of a disabled or chronically ill parent. Or even if only one parent raised you and that single mom or dad had to work extra shifts to keep the money coming in.

It may be that your family was poor, and you never knew real financial security. Or it could be you had a very large family and there simply wasn't enough parental attention or resources to go around.

But that was then, and this is now, right?

Well, sort of.

If you can't easily identify your needs, consider your past and the endless loops from childhood that are always playing through your brain. This is, of course, a habitual way of thinking that may have nothing at all to do with your current circumstances. It's thinking you may not be entirely aware of.

But then, that's how the subconscious is, right? It plays its dirge 24/7, and most of us are so used to it, we can't even hear it. We're like goldfish swimming in a dirty fishbowl that hasn't been cleaned for a while, so we swim ever more slowly. This is how we put up with all that pain and misery in the first place.

To paraphrase the wise Buddhist monk Thich Nhat Hanh, we prefer suffering simply because it is familiar. And yet, we can always stop choosing suffering. We can always opt for a freer, easier, more fulfilling way of life in which we get to relax and breathe instead.

We can always open our minds to something entirely different.

Be aware that vagueness is a great place to hide. Whether we can't decide where to go or we have no clue if we can actually afford a vacation or take the time off, the intent is the same. By staying vague, we leech out the crisp, confident energy of making a good decision.

We avoid the reality of making something happen. Instead, we stay stuck in the muck, because it's strangely comfortable in its discomfort. And yes, this is the "comfort" of overwork and suffering, which is simply unsustainable long term.

I invite you to explore a whole new way of thinking. I can promise you it may seem a little awkward at first. But do stick it out, friend, because it will deliver you to an infinitely better place.

First, I'd suggest you begin to actively tune in to your body. Wherever you are right now, close your eyes for a moment, put your feet on the floor, and take three slow, deep breaths. Then ask your body what you need.

Go ahead. Put this book down and try it right now.

Did thoughts swim into your mind? Perhaps even thoughts you didn't expect? If so, great work! If nothing happened, try the exercise again. Only this time, begin by taking ten slow, deep, conscious breaths. Then ask your body what you need. If you find yourself still resisting the process, ask yourself why, and wait for an answer to come up.

If you still get nothing, try again later. Just keep on trying because the answer—and your needs—will be forthcoming if you stick with it. In fact, the answer may swim up and surprise you when you least expect it. On the other hand, you could be immediately flooded with an awareness of a need you don't want to hear about. And if so, again, please hang in there.

Tensions, unresolved issues in life, points of pain, and various assorted sufferings may find you at moments like this. If they do, please bear with them, because they have important information for you. This is the voice of your heart speaking up, and it usually has a lot to say when given the chance.

Listen because the peace that prevails when you deal with these matters is profound. Once you do, you can relax into your life so much more completely. And then you will start to feel truly excellent.

Isn't the birthright of far greater happiness yours to claim as well?

Take a moment now to repeat the breathing exercise. This time, take five slow, deep breaths, and place one hand on your heart and the other on your belly.

Be present and make choices by listening to your body and soul. To do this, go lie on your bed, put your hands on your heart, and put the question out there. You will be guided.

—TEAL'S JOURNAL, SEPTEMBER 28, 2011

Take a few moments to answer this wonderful question:

What do I need right now?

Once you get in touch with your needs, ask yourself these questions as well. Don't overthink them or concern yourself with logistics. Just respond quickly and freely. Feel free to add any relevant notes as well.

What can I act on right now?

What can I act on in a few days to a week?

What can I act on in the coming months?

What am I afraid to act on?

eleven

how to ask for
what you need

. . . .

If you're like most people, you just came up with a very
specific need or even a list of them. But now you're going to
have to do something about those needs, right? This is where things
start to get complicated.

For instance, you might have to ask for something that makes you
uncomfortable. There may be people out there who don't want to
hear your request. And yet, make it you must. Because if you don't,
you're telling yourself you just don't matter.

(Do bear in mind you are free to request anything on the planet.
You may not get it, but you are certainly free to ask.)

On the other hand, maybe you don't feel particularly shy. Yet
you hold back because there seem to be so many more pressing
matters in your life right now, like all the busyness you need to
get to.

Again, this is just the illusion of overwork. If that old, familiar place of hiding once again calls you forth, do not heed its siren call, friend. It will not serve you well.

I've noticed over the years there are a number of ways we might avoid asking for what we need. Here's a brief list.

Ways People Avoid Asking for What They Need

Expecting others to read your mind. If you're patiently waiting for your spouse to quit leaving socks here and there, and he just doesn't get it, even though you pointedly glare at him each time you pick them up, please do yourself a favor. Just ask him to pick up his own damn socks. Be tough about it if you must, yet above all, be honest. You and your love both deserve it.

Deciding to deal with it later. I love "later." It's such a sweet fantasy. But "later" doesn't really exist, as opposed to, say, "next Tuesday at 4:00 p.m." Pick a precise time, calendar it, and make your request. This may seem silly, but try it anyway. It works.

Dropping hints. Hints do nothing but frustrate you, mainly because the person receiving them has no idea that they are hints. And that's because—again to Point 1—others cannot read your mind. It really is okay to be clear and ask for your need directly.

Promising yourself it's "just this time." Do you agree to things that fly in the face of your needs? Working late, for instance? Then you may tell yourself that "it's only this once." Which, of course, it isn't. Believing in illusions like this can be soul-crushing, not to mention a massive energy suck, and you deserve better.

Assuming you know what the answer will be, so you don't even ask. Assume nothing, my friend. And I do mean *nothing*. People can be wonderfully surprising. So just ask, all right? You never know.

. . .

Here's what's so surprising about all this. Requests are a two-way street. When you open up and make a request, you insert a little honesty and even intimacy into the relationship. Sure, it feels vulnerable. But it's also an excellent way to honor yourself and the other person.

For one thing, it says you trust him or her enough to tell the truth.

Then you give the other person a chance to give back to you. That's right; you give him an opportunity to step up, show what he's made of. And show you how much he cares. Are there those in your life who'd love a chance to do the same?

If you're in a relationship that's currently a bit grumpy and you risk some vulnerability when you make a request, you may be surprised to find things sweeten up quite nicely. Or you may get a reality check on the state of your relationship, and that may stir up a new, deeper set of needs. Either way, you will benefit from your newly found clarity.

Thich Nhat Hanh put it well when he noted that conflict is usually the direct result of misunderstanding. And that is why making a clear request is such a powerful thing to do. In an instant, all that misunderstanding can clear up before hurt feelings set in.

Bear in mind that the person receiving your request is under no obligation to say yes. A request freely made can and should get a yes or a no. Whatever the reply, *the key is not to take this reply personally.* Often what's going through the other person's mind are things we can't even fathom, most of which have nothing to do with us.

What's great is you are now clear. You are out of vagueness, and you are free to accept what's needed or move on to someone else with your request.

Simple, right?

How to Make a Powerful Request

As for making the actual request, there's a bit of an art to it, especially if it's a sensitive one. I've boiled this process down to four basic steps.

1. **Get clear on what you need.** If you need to journal on it before-hand, go right ahead. Check in with your body and see what it has to say about it. If you're a spiritually minded person, check in with your Higher Power. Or take what I like to call a "thinking walk," just a time to meander and ponder as you go.

2. **Once you are clear on your request, write it down** in a single, powerful sentence. It should look something like this: "I would like to _____" or

"Would you please _____?"

Make sure you know whom you need to ask.

3. **Pick the right time.** That would not be at the end of the day at work, when people are trying to leave. Nor would it be during your spouse's weekly football fest. Nor should it be when people are harried, busy, or stressed. Instead, choose a time when people are upbeat and relaxed. This may occur spontaneously, or it may have to be scheduled. It may even require a lunch or dinner in a nice restaurant. You'll know. Just be aware that timing is key. Then be willing to wait for the response. The other person deserves to have the time to think and respond appropriately.

4. **Keep it simple.** When making your request, do not preamble for ten minutes with a lot of extra talk, and don't try to leap in with a lot of reasons why saying yes is such a good idea. Instead, begin simply: "I was wondering if I could make a request..."

Then let the actual request hang in the silence once you've asked, no matter how strange or awkward that may feel. Let that silence do its work for you. This will give your request the weight it deserves.

You are back in your feminine
energy. Receive your feelings, keep
your intentions strong and present,
and act on what you want and feel.

—TEAL'S JOURNAL, SEPTEMBER 25, 2011

..... F I V E   M I N U T E S .....

The Tricky Request Worksheet

Write down your request as simply as possible.

Whom do you need to ask?

When would be the best time to do this?

Good job! Now go schedule it on your calendar.

twelve

what happens when we don't set good boundaries?

....

As I was saying earlier, sometimes somewhere along the way, our boundaries turn into Swiss cheese.

You know what I mean if you got bad at saying no and now the entire world seems to want something from you. But take heart, friend. There are direct and even kind ways to set a limit, and we'll get to those in a bit.

For now, let's take a closer look at boundaries in general. Boundaries are those invisible barriers our bodies, hearts, and souls tell us to set with people and situations when we're being intruded upon too much. Boundaries keep us relaxed, happy, and serene.

Boundaries also keep us safe, physically and emotionally. And some of us are much better at setting them than others. If you took care of everyone as a kid and have always been "the responsible one," your boundaries may need special attention. This is also true if you hate to speak up for yourself.

You can tell when a boundary is being violated because an uncomfortable feeling starts to creep up the back of your neck or take hold of your gut. Or an invisible sign in your brain starts flashing red, on and off.

Bottom line: you just *know*.

And yet, if you tend to be eager to please, you will ignore those signals and go along with pretty much anything anyone asks. That's how poor boundaries develop. We just want to be nice, often out of genuine compassion or a desire to help. Yet that's when an unfortunate dynamic kicks in, and suddenly, we find we're doing everything for everyone except ourselves.

You know your boundaries are being violated if a situation or a person leaves you feeling:

- Weak and powerless
- Inexplicably furious
- Resentful and generally annoyed
- Unable to protest or express a need
- Exhausted
- Impatient
- Grumpy

Or perhaps you find yourself complaining to those who can't actually help you in the situation.

Take a look at the following checklist and see if anything seems familiar.

..... THIRTY MINUTES .....

Your Boundary Violation Checklists

Imagine one or more recent experiences when you didn't set good boundaries or at the very least found yourself feeling resentful. Keep them in mind as you check those boxes that apply to you on the following checklists.

When I agree to something I don't want or need, I tell myself:

☐ "Somebody's got to do it. Might as well be me."

☐ "Let me just do it myself. That will be the fastest."

☐ "If I don't do it, I won't seem like a team player."

☐ "I have to work late. It won't be good enough if I don't."

☐ "I have to work late. It won't be finished if I don't." *(This one usually accompanies unreasonable time demands made by a boss.)*

☐ "I have to do it! I need the money/clients/customers/exposure." *(This may seem especially familiar if you are self-employed or a business owner.)*

☐ "If I don't do this, I'll never get a decent performance review/raise/bonus."

☐ "I have to do this. Everyone is counting on me!"

☐ "This'll only take a few minutes." *(Notice if you tell yourself this before a task that takes considerably longer.)*

☐ "I'm the only person qualified enough to do this." *(Is this really true?)*

☐ "If you want something done right, you've got to do it yourself."

☐ "No one's going to do this if I don't." *(Take note, compulsive volunteers.)*

☐ "Just get through this. It's no big deal."

☐ "This is the ONLY time I'm ever doing/going along with this (even though I secretly know it's not)."

☐ "As long as everyone else is happy, I'm good."

☐ "I just want to keep the peace."

☐ "It won't take that long. Just do it."

☐ "[INSERT NAME] will be so pleased if I just grit my teeth and do this."

☐ "Someday, I'm going to change my life, and no one will ever ask me to do this again."

Now add some of your own:

When I agree to do something I don't want or need, I feel:

☐ Pity

☐ Fear

☐ An intense desire to impress

☐ Overwhelming obligation I cannot shirk

☐ Compassion

☐ Desperation

☐ Trapped but unable to say no

☐ Alone

- [ ] Unsupported
- [ ] Unwilling but I do it anyway
- [ ] Aware of what I'm doing
- [ ] Confused
- [ ] Numb
- [ ] Lost
- [ ] A scrambling for control
- [ ] ....
- [ ] ....
- [ ] ....
- [ ] ....
- [ ] ....
- [ ] ....
- [ ] ....
- [ ] ....
- [ ] ....
- [ ] ....

When I agree to do something I don't want or need, I believe:

- [ ] It's my job regardless of how I feel.
- [ ] I can't ask for help.
- [ ] I don't need help.
- [ ] I am superhuman.
- [ ] My feelings are dangerous.
- [ ] I don't count.
- [ ] Everyone else's needs are more important than my own.
- [ ] I can't trust others.

- ☐ I will only be safe if I do it myself.
- ☐ I have no choice.
- ☐ Others will be impressed.
- ☐ I am stuck with this. There is no way out.
- ☐ ....
- ☐ ....
- ☐ ....
- ☐ ....
- ☐ ....
- ☐ ....
- ☐ ....
- ☐ ....
- ☐ ....
- ☐

Use what you learned from these checklists to journal on these questions.

How do you know when you need to say no?

Whom do you need to say no to?

When will you do this?

What will you say?

thirteen

the art of conscious decision-making

....

Let's now consider an alternative to blurting out the automatic, reflexive, boundary-destroying "Sure! I'd love to."

The mistake most of us make at such moments is that we don't take the time to make a conscious decision. We don't slow down and really listen to ourselves as we make that choice, mainly because we don't think we can.

And yet, that whip-fast yes has the power to upset our internal alignment. Every time we agree to something we don't want to do, our souls gets dinged a little. And those dings add up, until our emotional fenders are filled with them and we have become very weary indeed.

The solution is making conscious decisions, which can be new and different for some of us very hard workers. Instead, we often impulsively agree without thinking something through. Or we rush to a decision to move a certain choice off our desk or table. We tell ourselves we don't have time to deliberate, that something has to happen immediately. And yet, that is often far from the truth. Meanwhile, this is often the moment when our schedules become clogged with too much to do.

Conscious decisions are made, first and foremost, by listening to yourself. You alone hold the key to your internal alignment. And that alignment is the first priority when decisions are consciously made.

Here is a process for assessing each decision that comes your way and then answering in a way that takes care of you first.

When someone makes a request:

1. **Say "Let me think about this for a moment."** Heck, you can even get back to them tomorrow or in a few days. Avoid the impulse to minimize what you're agreeing to and give a fast yes. Instead, consider that this request is merely the beginning of a process in which you'll reply, but only when the time is right.

2. **Assess your immediate response.** What does your body say? What's your gut instinct? Trust your natural knowing, even if it's a flat-out no. Notice if you're trying to talk yourself into a different response.

3. **Pause and think about what's possible logistically.** Is there actually enough time to suit your needs if you agree? Is there enough support? Are there enough resources?

4. **Decide if you *want* to do it.** The more we actually honor our desires, the more consistent we are with our own energy and internal design. We were put together with our own particular tastes and desires for a reason, because they are what make us hum along nicely.

5. **Ask yourself if it fits with your values.** Self-care is ultimately about living your values. If you value being compassionate or helpful, and your own needs are not intruded upon by the request, why not do it? By the same token, listen to yourself if you are taken aback by *any* aspect of the request, including how it was asked.

6. **Determine what this will cost you.** Everything comes with a price, whether it's actual cash outlay or time and energy spent that could be better spent on something else. Weigh the pros and the cons once more.

7. **Ask yourself if there is a compelling reason to say yes.** Sometimes things look so-so on paper, but there's one big reason why certain requests should get a yes. These reasons are often intuitive, per the second point on this list.

Once you live with conscious decision-making for a while, you may notice yourself agreeing to do less and less but loving your life more and more.

And that's the point.

The Conscious Decision-Making Worksheet

Take a moment to put a decision on the table and think about it. Use the following worksheet to get more clarity and make a really conscious decision. Journal on each of these questions or even just the ones that seem most relevant to you.

What was your first reaction when asked to do something?

Would doing this be fun?

Would you have the time to do a focused, relaxed job if you said yes?

**Would you have to give something up
to make time or space for this request?
If so, are you willing to do so?**

If there is expense involved, can you afford it?

**Will this affect your health or your stress
level in a negative way? A positive way?**

**On a scale of 1 to 10 (1 is low, 10 is high),
how much do you want to do this?**

Is a yes here consistent with your values?

If it's more of a no, what's the problem?

Look over your answers to the preceding questions, and then journal for a few more moments on this question:

What have you just consciously decided and why?

fourteen

how (and why) to say no professionally

....

Some of us struggle mightily with saying no at work, usually because it just doesn't feel safe. This is when we find ourselves doing any number of avoidance dances.

We might cave in and give a yes when we don't mean it. We may procrastinate until the cows come home or slip out a back door whenever the requester comes our way. We may get all passive-aggressive and *reluctantly* say "Okayyyy" with a sigh, or keep changing the subject in meetings.

We may even hide behind closed doors or somehow subtly sabotage the project.

Hell, we might even call in sick.

We have all manner of subterfuges to avoid saying the dreaded word: no. After all, isn't the customer/boss/board of directors/

immediate superior always right? Shouldn't they be able to ask for whatever they want whenever they want it?

Actually, no. Not always.

By the same token, some of us say yes all the time out of the misguided belief that we really can't say no. We think the world demands that we stay glued to our desks and that we have no say in the matter. We tell ourselves no one else could possibly do the job we can do! Or we decide this is (yet another) emergency—it really has to get done now.

And true, sometimes, there are emergencies. But sometimes, that's just our mental chatter.

While it's important to be of service to people and have a good attitude, this premise can get stretched pretty thin, especially if it leaves us so depleted we can't actually perform our job well, and we burn out over time.

Working on weekends is a perfect example. There are those of us who do it without thinking. We have to go in on a Saturday, we tell ourselves. Nothing will get done otherwise! We tell ourselves we love how silent the office is, and we rejoice at how much work we get done.

Meanwhile, our souls are silently languishing, remembering the children we left at home or the time off we badly need.

And yet, what if you shut your office door during the week and hung a *Do Not Disturb* sign instead? What if you had someone else answer all those calls or just let them go to voicemail so you could take them at the right time? Imagine all the work you could get done during office hours.

What if you created interruption-free work time zones for yourself during the week? Or you arranged to work from home or another place where you could control the interruptions?

When you get right down to it, that burning question your colleague has can usually wait. The same with many of the dramatic problems that feel like they must be solved in the moment. Notice if people tend to congregate near your door or, worse, hang out in your office. This could be a sign that you are making yourself too available.

Again, here is where you have to ask yourself this question. Are you overproducing in an effort to be available all the time? Can you simplify your life by delivering just enough instead?

Great self-care begins with shoring up your resources and understanding how to advocate for yourself so you get your own needs met first. We're not talking about selfishness here. We're talking about self-preservation.

If you're a business owner and a client is only available to meet with you during your time off, you can consider adding an extra (hefty) fee for your time that really gives you some incentive. Or you can refer them to another provider who does work on the weekends. You can also reschedule your downtime, making sure to block it out on your calendar, and use it when the time arrives.

If your boss demands you "be part of the team" and work overtime, then you have to examine the office culture. Are you just going along with what everyone else does, even though it grates on your soul? And does this look like a dangerous pattern that threatens to become entrenched? Or perhaps it is already?

If so, it would be an excellent act of self-care to sit down with your boss and have a boundary-defining chat. You will then learn more about how well this particular job suits the empowered person you actually are. Is this job, with its culture of overwork, sustainable in your life? Does the joy of the work make up for its high costs?

Or is there a better, more perfectly aligned job just waiting for you out there?

On the other hand, are you creating the need to work extra hours in your time off out of your own demanding sense of perfectionism? (See the following chapter.)

What used to drive me to overwork was a haunting feeling that I'd never get ahead if I didn't work on the weekend. I missed my children's soccer games and an endless list of the things that make life sweet when I thought I had to work all the time. I regret that now.

Ultimately, I learned that all the noise in my head that kept driving me on was just an illusion. The work I was doing was actually good enough. In fact, it was better than good enough.

After my daughter's death, I discovered that nothing, repeat nothing, was as important as taking care of my own needs. Then I could really show up and be of service far more effectively. And that's when life got fun again.

I also discovered that when I didn't rush in to solve problems, other people did instead. And they got the chance to show up and save the day while I quietly put myself back together. The world did, indeed, go on.

Get in touch with the fire in your heart,
and you are strong and powerful!

—TEAL'S JOURNAL, SEPTEMBER 25, 2011

Now, about the actual saying of the professional no, there are several good ways to do this. First of all, be clear in your wording. Don't hide out in vagaries, like "I'll get back to you." Instead, be bold. Say "I'm sorry, I can't help you out" or "I'd love to, but I can't." Even "Not this time" will work.

This will feel strange at first and even uncomfortable if you're used to agreeing or volunteering all the time. But hang with it. This is where the gold is.

If you think your answer is a no, but you're unsure, you can say "Let me think about it" or even "Hang on a sec" for a quick, on-the-spot assessment. If you need more time, "I'll get back to you" works well.

Then be sure to get back to your requester, because each time you issue that conscious yes or no, you add a little more esteem to your personal bank.

Ultimately, your only job is to answer honestly, to advocate for yourself, first and foremost.

That, my friend, is real self-care, and it's the kind that lasts.

* * *

Journal on the following questions until you have reached clarity.

Whom do you need to say no to at work?

What's been stopping you?

What will you do about this?

When?

fifteen

to hell with perfectionism

. . . .

This just in: we are imperfect. Every last one of us, always and forever.

And here's the great news. Within that imperfection actually lies our perfection. If this sounds like a word puzzle, it's not.

It's just a bit of gristle the universe has given us to work with.

I say this as a recovering perfectionist. I've seen how ragged I've run myself throughout my life. All, of course, in the pursuit of that invisible ghost: perfection.

But when upheaval happens, you are suddenly forced to stop and let go, and then the truth dawns. There actually is no book of standards you must live up to. And the only person cracking that whip is you. For here lives perfectionism, the not-so-distant cousin of overproduction.

It wasn't until Teal suddenly died that I stopped trying to be a heroic superwoman. Because frankly, in the midst of my grief, there didn't seem to be much point.

Now I have a different perspective. I have decided to give myself all the time in the world to produce my writing, my talks, and my programs. I also give myself all the permission in the world to be gloriously imperfect.

This means I can mess up, make mistakes, and not get things right. Then I can ask for help, get feedback, correct course, and improve. And I can do this again and again and again. And it's okay!

Not only is it okay, it's remarkably fun as well.

I recently experienced this with a novel I had just finished writing. I asked a friend to read the first draft, knowing her analytical mind would pick up all kinds of loose ends in my complex plot.

She came up with a long list of fixes, all of which were feasible. After the list was delivered, what I felt was pure gratitude and some relief. I had known there were missing pieces in the book, but I wasn't sure what they were. Hallelujah!

Hours later, it suddenly occurred to me that my inner perfectionist hadn't even flinched. (She's the one who used to hate criticism.) The first draft wasn't a glowing model of perfection. The book needed work. And beautifully, that was okay! Bottom line is that my novel will now be vastly improved, so this is actually very good news.

In the old days, my perfectionist would have been appalled. It needed me to be impressive at everything I did the minute it was accomplished. Lord, that was tedious...and exhausting! It was an ancient mindset locked in place when I was a child by an encouraging father who frequently expected too much from me.

No one ever said to me, "Go ahead and be mediocre, honey. That's just fine." Instead, I was expected to be a star, and it was up to me to figure out how to do it.

Perfectionists, take note. Somehow, somewhere in our pasts, our little survivor selves believed we must overachieve to get our basic needs met. Perhaps you know what I'm talking about.

This would be you if you look in the mirror and see only flaws. If you worry, like I recently did, that your hair isn't perfect enough for a trip to the grocery store. Thankfully, I caught myself doing this. Then I could remind myself it was only a trip to Berkeley Bowl, not a world stage I was appearing on. Hair that was less than perfect was actually just fine.

The way around perfectionism is to shift the context of your work. Move each project from being a breathtaking act of flawless perfection to being, perhaps, an experiment. Or a study in what's possible. Or a good first stab or rough draft or whatever you need to call it to take the pressure off.

Decide your hair or your body or your outfit is just fine right now. And perhaps later, you'll do something about it, if you feel like it.

Make your current effort good enough for now.

Or possibly good enough. Period!

This may be uncomfortable at first, but trust me. You'll benefit in the long run. For one thing, you'll finally be able to relax, and that is a supreme act of self-care.

For me, this happened gradually in the course of all the various self-care actions I took. It was as if I was waking up from a deep sleep, looking around, and finally seeing the truth of my efforts.

The big thing I noticed was that I wasn't so bad after all and that my criteria for "just okay" was most people's criteria for "really, really good." In other words, I could finally recalibrate what I expected from myself.

Once I did this, I began to finally, truly enjoy my work.

Today, I keep the following promises with myself:

- Good enough is just fine with me, which may be less than I've delivered in the past.
- Mistakes ultimately make things better.
- Ask for help the minute you need it.
- There's plenty of time to get things done.
- Life is a process, so go with the flow.

Most of all, I keep in mind that if I don't do things perfectly the first time, the sky will not fall. In fact, I know I will be just fine, just as I have always been. And, of course, the same applies to you.

Perfection is nothing more than the cry of a frightened soul trying to get our attention. When we stop to listen to this voice and we reassure her that we're actually doing fine, then we relax. And ultimately, we grow.

For it is our compassion toward ourselves that really unlocks our brilliance, one sweet, vulnerable step at a time.

All we have to do is be willing to see the truth.

Are You a Perfectionist?

As you cruise through these questions, put down the first response that comes to mind. Don't overthink it.

When I begin a task or a project, I usually expect a perfect outcome from myself regardless of the circumstances.

   a. Often

   b. Sometimes

   c. Seldom

   d. Never

When I make a mistake, I experience panic or shame.

   a. Often

   b. Sometimes

   c. Seldom

   d. Never

When things don't turn out as I expected, I double down my efforts to "correct" the situation as quickly as possible.

   a. Often

   b. Sometimes

   c. Seldom

   d. Never

I'm uncomfortable with the idea of experimentation in tasks or projects.

    a. Often

    b. Sometimes

    c. Seldom

    d. Never

I secretly believe no one can do a given task or project as well as I can.

    a. Often

    b. Sometimes

    c. Seldom

    d. Never

I'm known as a tough boss or coworker, and I expect an enormous amount from the people on my team or close to me.

    a. Often

    b. Sometimes

    c. Seldom

    d. Never

I have a reputation for not giving my team or coworkers enough time or resources to get things done easily.

    a. Often

    b. Sometimes

    c. Seldom

    d. Never

I'm known as the team member to whom everyone turns to burn the midnight oil or get the job completed.

    a.   Often

    b.   Sometimes

    c.   Seldom

    d.   Never

I have a reputation for overdelivery. I may also have a feeling or a history of being underpaid or overworked.

    a.   Often

    b.   Sometimes

    c.   Seldom

    d.   Never

I'm the last to leave or the first to arrive in my work many days.

    a.   Often

    b.   Sometimes

    c.   Seldom

    d.   Never

I have trouble allowing enough time to get tasks and projects done with ease and grace.

    a.   Often

    b.   Sometimes

    c.   Seldom

    d.   Never

Somehow no matter how hard I work, the results are usually not good enough or satisfying to me.

a. Often

b. Sometimes

c. Seldom

d. Never

I avoid asking for help. It just seems easier to handle things myself.

a. Often

b. Sometimes

c. Seldom

d. Never

When I look at my work, I notice mostly the flaws, and they bug me for a long time to come.

a. Often

b. Sometimes

c. Seldom

d. Never

I have a nagging sense of "not enough" in general in my life, in terms of time, money, love, and overall satisfaction.

a. Often

b. Sometimes

c. Seldom

d. Never

I can still remember mistakes I made years ago, and I still feel shame about them.

   a. Often

   b. Sometimes

   c. Seldom

   d. Never

I am actually very competitive and take a lot of pride in being the best.

   a. Often

   b. Sometimes

   c. Seldom

   d. Never

It's important to me that people know I am the best at what I do. I'm not sure who I'd be otherwise.

   a. Often

   b. Sometimes

   c. Seldom

   d. Never

My response to criticism of my work is usually dread.

   a. Often

   b. Sometimes

   c. Seldom

   d. Never

I was raised by a parent or parents who expected an enormous amount from me. I never wanted to disappoint them.

   a. Often

   b. Sometimes

   c. Seldom

   d. Never

I have trouble completing projects.

   a. Often

   b. Sometimes

   c. Seldom

   d. Never

I can't seem to clearly define or get started on the work of my dreams.

   a. Often

   b. Sometimes

   c. Seldom

   d. Never

Now take a look at your answers. Are you surprised by any of them? Journal for a few minutes on the following questions.

Are you, in fact, a perfectionist?

Where could you ease up on yourself?

**What is something reassuring you could tell
yourself the next time perfectionism lurks?**

**What are three mistakes you've made,
and what did you learn from them?**

sixteen

how to say no to the people you love

....

For some of you, setting limits at work is no biggie. You can easily slip out at five every day, and you never even think of working on the weekends. You even ask for raises and get them with relative ease.

But at home, your usual resolve goes to hell. When your partner gives you that look—perhaps it's the one that melts your heart—you find yourself agreeing to yet another vacation with your mother-in-law. Or maybe it's a not-so-nice look you'd do anything to avoid.

On the other hand, it could be the kids making demands or even your own parents.

On the home front, an even more nuanced approach to saying no is often needed. Because basically, you love these people. You don't want to disappoint them when they make requests.

You might even be caught in years-long patterns of denying your own needs and caving to the desires of your family. You may have been taught this by your own mother if she was in those generations who were all about Mom the martyr.

You might have forgotten long ago who you really are and what you need in your closest relationships.

If so, please remember, you, too, get a say in how life is done. You, too, can say no to kids who ask relentlessly for money or sleepovers or new Xboxes or PlayStations. You, too, get to watch what you want to watch on TV sometimes. You, too, get to go flop on the couch while someone else does the dishes.

I know, I know. This message has been around a long time, yet even today, it bears repeating. And it may sound petty, especially if you're a mother and accustomed to taking care of everyone else, but you really do have to win a few once in a while.

A very wise psychologist said to me as I was about to marry my former husband, "It'll work out, as long as you both win a few." This is still my rule of thumb when it comes to getting along with family.

Every last little need of yours may not get met at home, but as long as most of them or even a good number are, you should be good to go.

As for how to actually say a conscious yes or no, the same rules as at work apply here. The only caveat is to remember that you're talking to the people you love. Deliver the yes or no with appropriate kindness and respect, just as you would like to be treated yourself.

Then allow yourself to be surprised. Sometimes the people closest to you can delight you in unexpected ways.

Finally, bear in mind that at home, you can get caught in such long-entrenched habits, you may not even realize you need to make a request. Take a look. Is there someplace in your personal life where your soul is chafing and you are yearning to break free?

That means you have an opportunity to make a kind yet firm request. Use the following questions to get clarity as to what you may need to ask for and from whom.

Remember I have the power to say no. If I feel myself closing down, look at whether I need to say no to something.

—TEAL'S JOURNAL, NOVEMBER 29, 2011

With whom do you need to set limits in your personal life?

What would you like to request?

When will you request it?

the joy (and relief) of getting mad responsibly

....

I don't know about you, but I hate getting mad.

I learned this after Teal's death. Along with my grief rode a side-car of toxic, bitter anger. I found myself becoming furious at small, irrational things. Yet again and again, I felt ashamed of these dark failings. But was my anger really a failing? Or was it actually all right?

As it turns out, my anger was a natural part of my grief. It was necessary—the sign of something stirring in the dark, narrow passageways of my grief. My anger was the ghost just down the way, beckoning for me to come hither and learn more.

Even Elisabeth Kübler-Ross said I was supposed to be mad.

Still, I hung back fearfully at first. I found myself pushing my anger away with platitudes instead of actually embracing it. Did I even have the energy for this? I wondered. Finally, I could avoid it no longer. That was when I discovered it was not only okay to get mad. It was necessary.

Just like a cool breeze on a hot day, when I finally allowed myself to feel my anger and journal on it, it refreshed and restored me. My anger literally healed me and became just as critical to my well-being as clean water, rest, and the great outdoors.

I moved on in far greater peace once I began to own all my feelings, including the less attractive ones.

If you are like me, you were raised to believe that anger is bad and good girls never get mad. So for the next forty years, I stuck my fingers in my ears and avoided such things. This is how we grow up numb and afraid to own or even know our anger...until it comes exploding out of us in unexpected ways.

From time to time, my own anger would explode, of course, and this filled me with a deep and abiding shame. Because I never learned how to handle my anger in a conscious way, I ran from it, afraid.

But you can learn to work with your anger. It simply takes a little practice.

First, you have to own it. Then you must actively stop yourself before you lash out, hurl invectives, or get into a snarl with someone. Tempting as it may be, this behavior will just create greater stress in your life.

The way of self-care is to stop and walk away when you feel like you're about to explode. This requires some self-control, but the rewards are well worth it. Once you have some time by yourself, you can stop and feel what is going on.

Allow yourself enough time to check in and assess what's wrong, even if it's only for a few minutes. (True self-care advocates will allow themselves as much time as they need here.) Notice where you feel your anger in your body.

Ask yourself what this anger of yours feels like. What other feelings might be present as well? What does it remind you of from your past?

Don't wander down the lane of your story and its inherent drama, and try not to imagine a million worst-case scenarios or vindictive triumphs. Instead, just do your best to stay present, sit with your emotions, and really feel them. They won't last long. Ideally, they will peak, crest, and then blessedly dissipate within a matter of minutes.

If anger is an unfamiliar or scary emotion, you may need to do a bit of journaling to process this. But hang with it, because this is when the healing happens. Don't let yourself get caught in the trap of believing such activity is a waste of time.

Your anger is not only righteous, it's a sign that your boundaries may have been violated or that something is really wrong. Don't brush that critical warning system away. Instead, allow it to bubble up in all its glory and prepare to learn from it.

For serious anger, take a big pad of oversized paper and scrawl on it furiously with a fat marker. Say everything you need to say... on paper. Use up the whole pad if you want. Really have at it until you're done. Then take that pad of paper, tear it up, and throw it away or even burn it. Say a few words of release if rituals of this type are your thing.

One way or another, get that toxic anger out of your body, out of your mind, and out of your space. And as ever, if you are left with disturbing, persistent, or dangerous thoughts or it is hard to work the anger through your system, get help. I found the right therapist tremendously healing in this effort.

Sometimes this is what it takes to let that massive freight train of your emotions move through you. Once your anger has come and gone, then life can go on and your whole central nervous system can relax. And then you will relax far more deeply, which feels incredibly great!

Only when you have real clarity and you've let off some steam should you have a conversation with those who've bugged you. Ideally, this is an intentional, firm but polite chat in which you express your needs and your requests.

Then you can move forward in peace and not hate yourself or anyone else afterward, regardless of the other person's reaction, for you know you will have taken the high road and acted for the highest good.

This is exactly how I've come to trust my anger and watched my base energy turn from worry and petty annoyance to clear, unimpeded happiness. As I moved through my anger at various situations and people, I began to realize a lot of my anger ultimately had to do with my own actions.

Once I vented my anger on paper, a new level of clarity descended, and I began to see a startling pattern. My anger at others was also partly anger at myself, for in many of my conflicts, I was responsible for at least part of the problem.

In certain tough relationships, I had been silent about my needs or willing to play the victim, and I hung on to resentments long after their due date. I began to take responsibility for my part, and then my anger turned to out-and-out forgiveness of myself and the other guy.

That's when I began to experience deep and lasting empathy.

When handled correctly, anger and the lessons it brings can be a balm to the soul. It is the release of the pressure valve and the surrender of the false veil that has us parked in "Everything is fine!" mode all the time.

Our anger tells us when things are out of balance. It's a highly sensitive internal warning system that tells us where to set boundaries and how to avoid danger and generally protect ourselves. In fact, it's a critical source of the information we need to grow and expand.

May you learn to enjoy your anger when it bubbles up and honor it for the innate and powerful wisdom that it is.

····· **FIFTEEN MINUTES** ·····

What Are You Mad About?

In the interest of clearing out the pipes, see if you can close your eyes and get in touch with at least one source of lingering anger. Then allow yourself to spend a little time with the process described earlier in the chapter.

Your heart deserves to be heard.

List your resentments here.

What was my part in this situation, if any?

eighteen
removing drama
from your life

. . . .

Now that you've handled perfectionism and anger, why not get rid of any drama in your life as well?

Here's the thing about drama. It pollutes the streams of life and gets in the way of you being in perfect, easy flow. And it doesn't like self-care one bit.

By drama, I mean those mini crises that filter through your life. The inexplicable need to help the alcoholic relative who's a hot mess most of the time. Or the attachment to the on-again, off-again relationship. Or the car that doesn't start half the time.

Such dramas may have been useful in the past, when they got your adrenaline going in that old familiar way from childhood. And yes, dramas are an effective way to divert attention from what's really going on with you. But who really needs all that Sturm und Drang?

Certainly not you.

You signed up to take better care of yourself, right?

When you really start to take loving care of yourself, dramatic people and situations begin to disappear. You'll notice this happening if the Negative Nelly who liked to stop by your cubicle and bitch suddenly stops appearing. Or if relatives who once leaned on you as the crisis master turn their attention elsewhere.

Why? Because once you get clear on how precious you, your time, and your energy are and you start setting appropriate boundaries and saying no, dramas no longer get to occupy your time. They become less interesting and even something to avoid. The same thing happens when you start to meet your own needs.

Then you can look at the car that doesn't start and decide it's time for a new one. Or you can check out your finances and decide you need a raise or a promotion. You can assess your energy level and decide you need a vacation.

You really can make the necessary changes that serve you. You just need to be willing to do it. Meanwhile, if your life is currently loaded with dramas, then it's a clear signal that it's time to focus on your own needs.

Ask yourself what areas of drama you would like to erase from your life. What can you do to shift the tension? Are there situations or even places you need to avoid? Or perhaps other people?

As for all those adults who claim to need your help, they are on their own healing journey, just like you are. So let the universe do its work, and get out of the way.

Allowing them to handle their own crises and dramas can feel strange and uncomfortable at first. It may even leave you feeling a little guilty. But that's okay. The ultimate serenity that will result is a great, great gift to yourself, one that will help you ultimately work less, contribute more, and feel a whole lot better about life.

Also, take note. You may be so oriented toward drama that you expect life to be complicated and difficult all the time. I experienced this recently when I had a sudden flat tire just as I was parking at the gym.

For a moment, I considered what to do. In the past, roadside assistance services had always taken so hellishly long, and hey, this was my precious workout time! But as I thought about what I really wanted, I decided I'd just go ahead and work out. Then I'd take my chances on getting the tire fixed afterward, even though it would be during rush hour.

Since I had a good book with me, I decided it was okay if the process took a while. Looking around, I realized it was actually a perfectly lovely evening in downtown Oakland. I knew I'd be just fine, so I left my flat tire and went to the gym and worked out. Then, an hour later and feeling refreshed, I called for help.

Literally four minutes later, the tow truck pulled up. A lovely young man named Andy jumped out, fixed my flat in eleven minutes, and chatted amiably throughout. Then I signed a form and off he went. Tire fixed. No biggie. I drove away with a smile on my face, happy I'd made the right choice.

I'd honored myself instead of the drama. Once again, peace prevailed.

This can either be a troubled time or a healing time. Let's make it a healing time.

—TEAL'S JOURNAL, SEPTEMBER 25, 2011

····· TWENTY MINUTES ·····

Where Does Drama Live in Your Life?

**List any situations where there is
currently tension or drama.**

What could you do about resolving the drama? Let your mind flow as you consider the possibilities.

nineteen
why (and when) it's a good idea to ask for help

....

Sometimes life's problems seem unsolvable.

It may seem like this when you're just too harried to think straight. Or when you feel clueless about where to even begin. This is when a bit of humility can serve you well. For not only is it safe to ask for help, it's usually a good idea.

There are, of course, caveats to this. You want to seek help from a trustworthy source, and you want to elicit the help you actually need. But before we get to all that, let's go over the basics.

You don't have to do it alone. Remember the Mary Oliver poem about crawling through the desert on your knees? This is what she was talking about. You, too, deserve support, even if you are a superwoman. (I'd say especially if you are a superwoman.)

You're not good at everything. You're just not. No one is. For me, this means I need help in the following areas: financial management, social media, my wireless network, anything requiring a screwdriver or a hammer, my car, my lingering allergies, some buried fears, tinkering with my blog, my tense shoulders, and my occasional insomnia. The list goes on and on. Once you decide to elicit help, not only does that part of your life improve, your entire life does as well. Try it and see.

P.S. Such help does not have to be paid help. Friends, neighbors, family members, support group pals, interns, and online mentors can be helpers too.

Emotional support is okay too. Sometimes we think the only type of support we *really* need is technical, health, or automotive. Yet what about our feelings? Our emotional life may have churned along in the background for so long we can't even see if there's trouble there. We're just aware of a dull ache somewhere. That's when it's a great idea to sort through things with a therapist, spiritual advisor, or even a life coach.

Group support gives you an extra boost. I love support groups, though frankly, I used to hate them. But then Teal died, the bottom dropped out, and I realized I needed all kinds of help. Since then, I found my way into recovery groups, spiritual groups, yoga groups, meditation groups, business networking groups, and even a group for grieving parents. Support groups give you two things—a place to share your story and a way to hear everyone else's. Then you realize you're not alone, and you can pick up valuable tips and resources. You may also befriend people traveling the same path, which is beyond precious. Groups bring community, and community is just plain essential.

Added support keeps you accountable. If you need support sticking with something difficult like a weight loss or addiction recovery, it really helps to have a group or a trainer/coach/therapist or even an action buddy to check in with. Then you have to show up and share your progress each week. You have a place to talk about or even email your challenges. So you build a team around you that is heading in the same, healthy direction. The sweet reality of accountability keeps you grounded in your work, and that's a great boon.

A final note: If you're a person who hates to ask for help, take heart. Asking for help does not in any way mean you are weak, unstable, or a loser. What it means is that you have the wisdom to know you can't do life alone, and therefore you will automatically up your game on all levels once you get more support.

Asking for help actually means you're strong and brave.

Don't be afraid to ask for something if you don't know what to do. You are capable.

—TEAL'S JOURNAL, SEPTEMBER 12, 2011

twenty
where to find
the help you need

. . . .

As for where to find that precious help, begin by assessing what sort you need. If you find that you really need to talk to someone about something sensitive, like your shaky marriage, one place to begin is with your personal network.

Is there a truly trusted friend or family member you can confidently—and confidentially—share with? Who's the first person who comes to mind?

Now ask yourself the hard questions: Will that person protect your privacy? Will he or she be a good listener or all too eager to bust in with too much advice? Is this person truly objective? Will the advice you are given be sound?

Sometimes we habitually turn to old friends or family members who might actually not be the best people to discuss things with. Take note if your body gives a sigh of happiness or your shoulders tense up when you anticipate the conversation.

If there isn't anyone readily available in your network, move on to seek professional help. I like online review systems like Yelp and Google reviews for assessing where to find therapists, doctors, nutritionists, coaches, consultants, and various advisors. Of course, you do have to vet those reviews and weed out the suspicious overly negative or overly positive voices.

On the other hand, a spiritual advisor such as your local pastor, rabbi, imam, or Buddhist teacher may be what is required. Even if you don't have a specific faith you practice, these people have pastoral care practices that are here for you. And who knows? If you get a nudge in this direction, you may find an entirely new community to join. Consider asking a friend who attends such services. Could they possibly help you find the right person for support?

Speaking of friends, sometimes what's needed is an action buddy. By this, I mean someone whose job it is to keep you accountable for the things you say you want to do. And you, in turn, keep them accountable. Maybe you set goals with one another and meet periodically for lunch. If it's not practical to meet live, there's always Skype, Zoom, FaceTime, or the good old phone to keep you connected as you work together. Or maybe you organize your thoughts into an email or text that you exchange every day.

Action buddies walk the road with you and lend support along the way. And not only are they extremely valuable, they are free. The key is to choose someone reliable with whom you resonate and who needs and offers support in equal measure. Note: You don't have to be working on the same sorts of things, but it can serve as valuable glue in the relationship if you do.

In turn, offering a quick shot of support to your buddy when needed can remind you of your grounding and your power and just be plain old good for your karma. My buddy and I simply exchange emails each workday morning, nothing more than that. It takes less than a minute, but somehow it really helps me stay on task and get things done. Also, because I list not only my actions for the day but also my self-care items, I see how balanced my day will be from the start.

It simply helps to know someone else out there is aware of what I'm up to each day. Occasionally, we even cheer each other on or offer resources or support.

There are also other kinds of buddies. Travel buddies come along for the ride when you are afraid to travel solo. Accountability buddies can help you stop procrastinating and get things done. Walking buddies keep you moving. And the list goes on and on. Buddies can be invaluable in pursuing dreams or bucket list items you just can't get to or possibly for exercise or volunteer activities you may not get to otherwise.

Also, consider this. If you know already that it will be hard to work self-care into your life, how about having a dedicated self-care buddy?

A great place to look for buddies is in groups you resonate with, whether that's a Meetup group, your yoga class, or a group at your church or temple. If you know you procrastinate or avoid moving ahead in a particular area, look for someone in a group related to that focus. Then imagine how great it would be to drop a text to a buddy who understands when you're about to, say, break your diet. All you might need is a quick word of encouragement to stay the course.

Don't forget the various types of twelve-step recovery groups, which are by no means limited to Alcoholics Anonymous. They cover everything from overwork, food, and financial addictions to codependency and relationship addiction. Groups such as Al-Anon are a terrific comfort if you have addicts in your life or you grew up with them. These meetings are loaded with people you might become buddies with as you work your program. Simply search on Google to find your nearest chapters and meetings.

Hospitals and hospices offer free support groups for people who are grieving or stressed, have specific health challenges, or are care-givers spending lots of time caring for family or friends. Many are here for you whether or not you have ever done business with them. I got eight free sessions with a grief therapist followed by three months of free group support from a local hospice after Teal died, which was hugely helpful.

Simply do an internet search to find what's meeting locally or online in your area of concern. Some groups meet in person. Some meet on the phone, using a conference line. Some meet online via services like Skype or GoToMeeting. What serves you? Think about how you like to communicate with others and what suits your personal style.

On the other hand, maybe the support you need is not related to a buddy or a group but is more logistical. Like someone to clean out your closets or wait in line for you at the DMV. That's where I love to use online services such as TaskRabbit. This is an online resource loaded with all kinds of temporary, one-gig-at-a-time helpers and workers. These folks are vetted thoroughly, and you can find help for nearly everything—from mowing your lawn to driving your mother to the dentist.

A fun site that provides more creative help can be found on Fiverr, many for the reasonable fee of $5. Here, the help runs the gamut. Vendors do everything from design your holiday or business card to cut your videos and upgrade your Tinder profile. For a little more, you can get faster or more complex services, like the person who puts your message on a gorgeous sandcastle and photographs it for a mere $10. Small businesses can find copious help here as well.

And hey, if you have kids in the house, it's not too late to tap them to contribute. Kids as young as six can (and should) be enlisted to help clean up, with simple tasks like emptying trash cans, dusting, and watering plants. Not only do tasks get done, but the kids learn something about responsibility and how the real world works. Older ones can help with household pets, vacuuming, taking out garbage and recycling, and cleaning bathrooms.

Some excellent ideas on how to mobilize the kids are in a classic book, *Children Who Do Too Little*, by Patricia Sprinkle. I've also found that if you make it a game, you'll get better results—especially if the children get to design the method for assigning tasks. One ingenious friend co-opted a spin dial from a board game into a new game, "Spin for Your Chores," and got her house cleaned in the process every week.

A Note for Those Who Can't Delegate

Are you afraid to, say, hire someone to clean up after your dinner party or organize your files? I know how you feel. I used to be afraid too.

But then I discovered how liberating taking that extra help can be. It's actually like taking a giant deep breath. Once you let go and allow that help in, everything starts to relax.

The key is to allow yourself to become uncomfortable with this prospect. Then just kindly, patiently talk yourself through the process, and don't give up. Check in with your buddy before and after you make the request. And allow yourself to feel good and vulnerable, for these feelings will certainly pass.

The result is that you can then settle into your day in a whole new, more easeful way, without these added pressures. Trust me on this. Getting help is seriously worth whatever discomfort it may cause.

Once more, I'm here to gently remind you that your job now is to focus on your self-care, even when it feels awkward or uncomfortable.

I promise. You can do it.

Do You Need a Self-Care Buddy?

Here's where we're going in this book. By the end, you'll have a clear list of self-care actions to take. Some will be everyday, regular tasks you'll build into your schedule, and others will be singular events, like apologizing to your ex or booking a cruise to Alaska.

Either way, it helps to have someone keep you accountable.

That's why I recommend having a self-care buddy you email or text each day with your list of the day's upcoming self-care tasks. Also include your self-care list from the previous day, with those items you completed marked off. Over time, you'll see which self-care tasks you tend to skimp or avoid and which ones you never miss. Then you can do some journaling to find out what your resistance is all about or what would serve you better.

You may even want to get together with your self-care buddy and enjoy some mutual R & R, like a trip to the day spa or a walk through the park. (Be sure to take a photo and send it to us at the Self-Care Group for Extremely Busy Women on Facebook! See page 134.)

And of course, you can return the favor to your beloved self-care buddy by receiving their list of self-care tasks each day, some of which may inspire more of your own. You don't have to do anything with this information. Just receiving it is enough, though it's always nice to add a note of encouragement in your email or text.

Having a self-care buddy is a perfect way to ground yourself in the practices of this book. And how do you find one? Just ask. Look in any relevant groups you belong to, as recommended earlier. Surely, right now, you can think of someone who needs self-care as much as you do. Whether they choose to read this book or not, they will understand the simple relief that comes with greater self-care. And the need for some accountability.

Take a moment now and jot down the names of a few people who might be perfect self-care buddies for you. Don't overthink it. Let your instinct guide you.

Self-Care Buddies:

twenty-one
whom to ask for help

····· TWENTY MINUTES ·····

Meander through this list, checking those boxes that apply to you. In the blanks provided, add anyone or anything not included that springs to mind. Then, after each section, organize your thoughts into whom you'd ask for help and what you need help with.

Feel free to return to this list as many times as you need to, and fill it in much more extensively.

Whom can you ask for help?

☐ Friends

☐ Family members

☐ Your spouse

☐ Your children

☐ Neighbors

☐ Community members

☐ ....

☐ ....

☐ ....

☐ ....

☐ ....

☐ ....

☐ ....

☐ ....

Feel free to add your own ideas or specific people here. Note what you'd ask them about as well.

Who?	For What?
Personal task helper or assistant	
Babysitter	
Bookkeeper	
Housekeeper	
Professional organizer	

Handyperson	
Cook, chef, or cooking teacher	
Gardener or lawn mower	
Builder or contractor	
Interior design	
Architect	
Real estate agent	
Painter	

Mortgage broker	
Financial planner or advisor	
Personal banker	
Stylist	
Hairstylist	
Dating coach	

Who?	For What?
Religious advisor	
Spiritual advisor	
Meditation teacher	

Who?	For What?
Office assistant	

Your boss	
Your employee(s)	
A professional mentor	
Accountant	
Bookkeeper	
Business consultant	
Executive coach	
Virtual assistant	

Who?	For What?
Massage therapist	
Personal trainer	
Chiropractor	
Dentist	

Doctor	
Naturopath	
Marriage and family therapist	
Psychiatrist	
Nutritionist	

Who?	For What?
Dance instructor	
Travel bureau	
Life coach	
Sports team or training group	
Yoga teacher	
Tai chi or martial arts instructor	
Craft instructor	

What groups would add greater support to your life?

First, how would you like to meet with your group?

☐   In person

☐   Online via Skype or other platforms

☐   By phone

What sort of group speaks to you?

☐   Meetup group (meetup.com)

☐   Twelve-step recovery group

☐   Grief group

☐   Continuing education class (cooking, language arts, creative skills, etc.)

☐   Online training

☐   Professional training

☐   Stress relief group

☐   Group therapy

☐   Meditation group

☐   Knitting or craft group

☐   Reading group

☐   Spiritual group (Buddhist sangha, yoga, etc.)

☐   Women's group

☐   Caregiver's group

☐   Group for people with specific health issue

☐   Healing group

☐   _____

☐   _____

- [ ]
- [ ]
- [ ]
- [ ]
- [ ]
- [ ]
- [ ]
- [ ]
- [ ]

What would you like to work on in the group?

Type of Group	Helping with What Issue?

Also, drop in and join us at our Facebook group, the Self-Care Group for Extremely Busy Women. It's a stick-together community where you can find the ideas, relief, reassurance, support, and everyday thoughts to keep you going on your quest for greater self-care. After all, these are your people—fellow extremely busy women who know they need more nurturing. I'm there often, answering questions, sharing insights, and generally spreading love and healing. Hope to see you there!

twenty-two

do you need a therapist or a life coach?

. . . .

It's murky, right? Yet there is a real difference between life coaches and therapists. And neither may be a fit for you. Still, both can be extremely effective in supporting your self-care.

Psychotherapists (also known as therapists or counselors) are licensed mental health professionals who use various techniques including talk therapy, trauma therapies like eye movement desensitization and reprocessing (EMDR), cognitive behavioral therapy (CBT), and other modalities to help you with your issues. They see themselves as perspective-shifting listeners who can help you thrive by asking questions, changing behaviors, or perhaps talking about your past in order to overcome current issues.

A psychotherapist can be very helpful for rooting out long-standing emotional problems and patterns, working on issues like addictions, depression, insomnia, or anxiety, or consulting on specific relationship, health, stress, or work challenges. You can find a broad range of therapists in your area by googling "Psychology Today therapist finder."

Life coaches are often, but not always, licensed professionals who tend to focus on helping you create present and future goals. Their tool kit includes many types of assessments (think career counselor surveys, for instance), as well as a broad range of planning, goal-setting, and personal development techniques. Just as athletes rise to their best with the right coach, so can you. Life coaches are generally hired by individuals.

Then there are executive coaches, who can be hired by organizations to help busy professionals and work teams clarify and achieve their goals and rise to their next level. Coaches can also be brought in to work on issues like team building, professional relationship skills, and breaking down all kinds of barriers.

Occasionally, executive coaches may consult on areas related to business performance, such as stress reduction, well-being, and resilience, so there may be some overlap with the domains addressed by life coaches. Executive coaches typically have experience in a particular industry.

A good directory of credentialed life coaches is available at coachfederation.org.

**Do you need a life coach
or a therapist?**

**What would you hire him/
her to work on with you?**

twenty-three
a brief word about your values

. . . .

Have you ever felt like you were drowning in obligations? If so, you are seriously not alone.

The key is to not let your commitments overrun you. But given that you are extremely busy women, there could be a real chance of that. So how do you fight off that urge to over-obligate?

Simple. Don't say yes so often.

This may mean you have to sit with some very uncomfortable feelings sometimes. It may mean you have to disappoint someone—maybe even your own child or the boss who scares you. It may mean you have to sit on your hands when nobody else in the room jumps in to help.

Ultimately, to really take care of yourself, you may have to redefine who you are in the world. Because when you get right down to it, obligations are really about values. If you are rigorous about what you agree to do, the things you truly, deeply care about rise to the top of the list. That's when you become far more effective and a whole lot happier. Meanwhile, the things that are less important simply disappear.

This is how we move from being harried to being centered, passionate, and free.

Getting clear on your values is a critical skill for extremely busy women. There really are only twenty-four hours in a day, eight of which should be spent asleep. That leaves sixteen hours to rock and roll. With whom will you share that precious time? And how much of it should be spent on yourself?

These are key essentials to consider when crafting a more conscious life of self-care.

I know some of the obligations we have cannot be changed. Mothering. Taxes. Dentists. House repairs. Critical but tedious work tasks. The list goes on, which is why it's even more critical to get clear on your values.

Here is a handy sorter that will help you begin to figure out what are the most important things in your life and which ones you are ready to let go of now.

If you feel your mind wandering to something inconsistent with you, thank it. Let it go, say it doesn't match with me, and get present.

—TEAL'S JOURNAL

····· THIRTY MINUTES ·····

The Handy Values Sorter

Write down the top twenty-five ways you spend most of your time.

1. ....
2. ....
3. ....
4. ....
5. ....
6. ....
7. ....
8. ....
9. ....
10. ....
11. ....
12. ....
13. ....
14. ....
15. ....
16. ....
17. ....
18. ....
19. ....
20. ....
21. ....

22. ....

23. ....

24. ....

25. ....

Now let's try a little visualization. Do this exercise when you have a bit of time to shut the door and relax.

After you read this, allow yourself to close your eyes, let go, and let your whole body relax as you **take five long, slow breaths.** Then think of a peaceful scene at the end of your life.

Really try to imagine it. See the people around you and the room in which you lie dying. Imagine yourself as an older person who has lived a good long life, and really feel the finality of the scene. *This is it.*

Then open your eyes after a moment and read on.

Look at the preceding list and cross out those tasks that simply don't matter. Don't stop and reason or think about the logistics of letting them go. This is only an exercise.

Go with your first impulse and cross out any tasks, people, or places that don't seem that important. If anything on the list really annoys you, be sure to cross it off as well.

Now pick the five items that are the most important ones in your life, and list them below. Then check off each one in the list on page 140.

1. ....
2. ....
3. ....
4. ....
5. ....

Pick the five items that are next in importance in your life, and list them below. Then check off each one in the list on page 140.

6. ....
7. ....
8. ....
9. ....
10. ....

Pick the next five items that are less (but still somewhat) important in your life, and list them below. Then check off each one in the list on page 140.

11. ....
12. ....
13. ....

14. ....

15. ....

Now list everything else, including those items you crossed off initially. Then check off each one in the list on page 140.

16. ....

17. ....

18. ....

19. ....

20. ....

21. ....

22. ....

23. ....

24. ....

25. ....

All the items on your initial list of twenty-five should be checked off at this point. The last ten items are the negotiable ones that can be let go of or kept with the understanding that they simply aren't as important as the first fifteen.

Use this information the next time you are asked to commit to yet another project. Is it more important than anything on this list you'd like to keep?

Also, take a look at your top fifteen items and ask yourself the following questions:

Is everything in balance? There should be equal parts of work and play, self-care, and taking care of life's business.

Are there any obvious gaps in your fifteen most important items? Is exercise missing? Or love?

What did you forget to add? Go in and tweak the list as needed. But notice if your mind gets harried and wants to add things out of fear or worry about what someone will think. Remember, your soul helped you write this list, and she is *always* worth listening to!

part two

self-care
essentials

twenty-four
essential #1: a good night's sleep

. . . .

I know, I know. You've got pressures. I've got pressures too. Sleep is hard, right?

You may have gotten to the point in your life when relaxing only happens late at night. Or maybe you've hit menopause, so your sleep has become erratic and difficult.

Yet a good night's sleep is literally what makes the difference between a life well lived and an existence you just drag yourself through.

Sleep is our emotional clearinghouse, where we silently resolve all that is churning in our psyche. Not only does your entire body need to rest and regroup each night, but you've got stuff to work out as well.

Whether it's worrying about work, starting a new relationship, or letting go of a beloved job, the inner wheels of your subconscious must turn.

If it's been a while since you felt that "Ah! It's great to be up in the morning!" feeling, here are some ideas for getting a good night's sleep. May they serve you well.

Avoid sugar and carbs. This is especially true once you get deep into menopause, when hot flashes and night sweats become your new reality. Most of them end when you take sugar out of your diet, especially if you add ground flaxseed to your diet. You can even go one step further, according to retired Bay Area gynecologist Rima Goldman, MD, and avoid all carbs in the evening. That would mean no pasta, rice, potatoes, or bread with dinner, in addition to avoiding sugar and sugary drinks.* This makes a remarkable difference.

Regulate sleeping hours. I got great value from a book about getting back to sleep by Gregg D. Jacobs, *Say Good Night to Insomnia.* His approach is very close to cognitive behavioral therapy for insomnia, which the Mayo Clinic recommends. One thing Jacobs really stresses is getting on a regular schedule that minimizes time in bed. The idea is to be asleep by 11:00 p.m., then get up with the light as you naturally waken. This plan discourages lounging in bed in the morning or catching up on the weekends. And it really has made a big impact on my own sleeplessness

Avoid screens ninety minutes before bed. Lord almighty, how I resisted this! But all the blue light that emanates from LED screens can affect our production of sleep-inducing melatonin and thus the sleep drive that keeps us resting peacefully. I finally turned off the

----

*   Notes from an unpublished interview, https://doctor.webmd.com/doctor/rima-goldman-02e86842-b976-4a9c-8b0b-7dd7a98a929b-overview.

TV a lot earlier than I used to, and I started taking books out of the library instead of reading myself to sleep with my iPad. And I stopped looking at my smartphone about an hour before bedtime.

Cutting out that ambient screen light for a few hours before bedtime seriously makes a difference. If you can't peel away from screens, you might also check out blue-light-blocking apps for the computer and smartphone, such as Night Shift on Apple's products.

Another option is to wear blue-light-blocking eyeglasses, sold on Amazon. These are yellow-tinted glasses that block out any blue light emanating from screens. I've found them to be remarkably effective.

Exercise regularly. I have tested this, and yep, it makes a difference. Get organized about your exercise, join a gym, start walking, or make a regular date at your yoga studio. If you can get your body moving five times a week, regular sleep will be much more likely. (See chapter 28, which covers exercise, to learn more about staying motivated.)

Avoid caffeinated coffee or tea. I know this may sound extreme, but trust me on this. If you're at all sensitive to caffeine, don't even drink it in the morning, or it could impact your sleep. Even strong decaf coffee or tea has some caffeine that can cause problems. And the same is true of chocolate, cocoa, and cacao (chocolate's powdered raw source). Instead, try decaf green or herbal tea or a good herbal coffee substitute like Teeccino (also sold online in some remarkably good flavors). It works.

Reduce or eliminate use of alcohol. This can be hard to give up, but doing so is also key to good sleep. Alcohol turns into a stimulant in the body that can kick in during the latter half of the sleep cycle or make it really hard to fall asleep in the first place.* One idea if you love your occasional glass of wine is only to drink a half glass. Or perhaps have it mid- to late afternoon so it has time to cycle through your body. You can even add ice to a single glass of white wine to make it last longer (my apologies to all wine connoisseurs). As you come to value good sleep more and more, you may just lose your taste for alcohol, not to mention a few pounds.

Take sleepy supplements. There are many out there, from relaxant GABA and mood enhancer 5-HTP to melatonin, which can be good for resetting sleep patterns during events like jet lag. According to Dr. Karen Kartch, who offers designed clinical nutrition services, a helpful homeopathic remedy that removes the anxiety related to insomnia is Hyland's Calms Forte.† In fact, there are too many sleep-inducing supplements to list here. The trick is finding which one works for you. There is an abundance of research of varying qualities on the internet about all of these. Consult with a physician or health practitioner before taking any supplements, especially if you currently take medications.

Meditate before bed or during the night. Whenever I can get myself to do this, it works. If screens don't bother you before bed, there are many popular apps that offer up soothing guided visualizations, such as Calm and Headspace. Insight Timer allows you to

---

*   Michael J. Breus, "Alcohol Likely to Keep You Awake, Not Make You Sleep," *Psychology Today*, February 4, 2013, https://www.psychologytoday.com/us/blog/sleep-newzzz /201302/alcohol-likely-keep-you-awake-not-help-you-sleep.

†   From private interview, Dr. Karen Kartch, http://kartchchiro.com/.

build your own timer with a variety of gentle background tracks and has an excellent library of guided visualizations. See my list of favorite self-care apps at suzannefalter.com/self-care-apps/ for a current list.

If you're trying to avoid screens at night, there's always just plain old sitting in silence. Try this in the middle of the night if you can't sleep; you don't even have to sit up. I like "beditation," in which I take myself through relaxing every part of my body as I lie there, eyes closed and breathing slowly. *Say Good Night to Insomnia*, mentioned earlier, has an excellent section on this.

Use sleep tracking apps. If you aren't avoiding screens at bedtime too rigorously, keeping track of the stats on your sleep can be helpful. Apps like Sleep Cycle track your sleep using the microphone in your smartphone. You keep the phone plugged in on a table next to your bed and run the app while you sleep. The app will track all sorts of information, including the depth of your sleep cycles. When it's time to wake up, Sleep Cycle will gently rouse you at the perfect moment in your sleep cycle, based on a window of wake-up times you provide. Now that's soothing!

Keep a sleep log. Take that information you gathered and track your sleep as you test various items on this list, from exercising and avoiding alcohol to taking assorted supplements and limiting screen time. Awareness of what works requires detail, so this helps a lot. *Say Good Night to Insomnia* has an alternative, written-out sleep log and recommendations for sleep tracking that don't require use of a smartphone or an app at night. Once you've accumulated enough information, you'll start to see patterns, and you can design your perfect support system for getting the sleep you need.

Read Ralph Waldo Emerson, something calming, or even something slightly boring. Experts advise getting out of bed, finding a cozy spot, and reading a calming book for no more than thirty minutes when you can't sleep. (That would be the paperback or hardcover variety.) However, I find if I wait a bit longer in bed, then I only read for a few minutes before I get sleepy. The key to this is repetition of routine. Note: Pick something low-key to read that won't engage your brain too much.

Use good earplugs. Not enough can be said about the importance of your sleep environment. If the dog scratches and it wakes you up or the blind gently taps the window frame on a breeze and you sit up, alarmed, try wearing earplugs. Silicone earplugs, which you can find online, can make all the difference.

Open (or close) a window. Sleep experts assert that cooler temperatures prove more conducive to sleep.* So open a window. (If it's noisy outside your window, don't forget the earplugs.) On the other hand, it could be too chilly in your bedroom, mainly because your body temperature goes down when you sleep. Ralph Downey III, PhD, chief of sleep medicine at Loma Linda University, says the comfort of your bedroom temperature directly affects how you move through your body's REM cycle during sleep.†

Don't forget that your body was designed for sleep, so many of

- - - - - - - - - - - - - - - - - -

*   Kazue Okamoto-Mizuno and Koh Mizuno, "Effect of Environment on Sleep and Circadian Rhythm," *Journal of Physiological Anthropology* 31, no. 1 (May 31, 2012): 14, https://www.ncbi.nlm.nih.gov/pmc/articles/PMC3427038/.

†   Kimberly Sayers Bartosch, "How to Design a Bedroom for Better Sleep," *Spruce*, August 8, 2018, https://www.thespruce.com/design-a-bedroom-for-better-sleep-350739.

these tricks are just meant to support a natural process that's already trying to happen.

Sweet dreams!

How Sleep Deprived Are You?

Spend a few moments filling out the **Epworth Sleepiness Scale**. You can find a handy PDF when you search for this online. This is the same test that sleep therapists give you to assess the severity of your sleep issue.

If you find you are in bad shape and none of the suggestions mentioned earlier work for you, I recommend finding a qualified sleep therapist who practices cognitive behavioral therapy (CBT) for insomnia. This behavioral modification program is said to be 85 percent effective and recommended by most MDs for insomnia, and it can be well worth the investment of time and energy.

I found my own sleep therapist by searching Yelp.com. Studies prove that working with a CBT sleep therapist is often more effective than sleeping pills in resolving insomnia.[‡]

- - - - - - - - - - - - - - - - - -

‡   Kirstie N. Anderson, "Insomnia and Cognitive Behavioural Therapy—How to Assess Your Patient and Why It Should Be a Standard Part of Care," *Journal of Thoracic Disease* 10, no. 1 (January 2018): S94–S102, https://www.ncbi.nlm.nih.gov/pmc/articles/PM C5803038/.

Build This into Your Life

When I think about what has really improved my sleep, the big one is tracking my sleep. Whether you choose to use an app or a sleep log, make your first task of every day to record how you slept.

The act of writing this down on a grid in a notebook can really help ground you in the reality of your sleep situation, and that will move you to look at why you don't sleep well. I've included a sample grid page that you can re-create or copy.

The answer may be obvious, i.e. you stayed up until one in the morning binging on Netflix. Yet perhaps you have a persistent sleep problem, in which case taking a detailed look at your sleep patterns and habits over time is crucial.

(Note your times for waking and sleeping approximately during the night, as looking at clocks is not recommended by sleep therapists.)

Track your sleep for two or three weeks, then determine what worked and what didn't. Notice if you have trouble regulating your sleeping and waking times and what your patterns of wakefulness are.

Record what worked and what didn't from the items in this chapter in the Notes section, as well as any external conditions such as noise, heat, the dog barking, hot flashes, etc. Write down whether you drank alcohol or had caffeine or chocolate close to bedtime, as well as any sleep supplements, sleeping pills, medical marijuana, etc.

Then keep playing with it. I found it was only after extensive experimentation that I really began to heal my insomnia. As long as you are clear on exactly what's happening at night and you respond to patterns you observe, you'll have a better chance of repairing your sleep.

Sleep Tracker

	Mon	Tue	Wed	Thu	Fri	Sat	Sun
Time to Bed							
Minutes to Fall Asleep							
Number of Wakes							
Total Time Awake							
Final Waking							
Time You Got Up							
Sleep Quality (1 to 5)							
Sleep Aids?							
Notes							

twenty-five
essential #2:
peaceful love

. . . .

We are generally a mating species, designed for companionship. Yet sometimes, for reasons we may not even fully understand, we prefer being alone for a while. Often, it has something to do with healing, and that's just fine.

When you have a peaceful relationship with love, you know what you're about. You are either happily ensconced with someone, busy dating, or tranquil in your aloneness. You don't spend your nights longing for that elusive Other. Nor do you gnash your teeth and resent your spouse while denying your own needs.

Love that's healthy is abundant, thriving, and free, as opposed to controlling, draining, violent, scary, addictive, or abusive in any way. It leaves you feeling safe, secure, understood, and appreciated each day instead of tired and beaten up. You know you can express yourself easily without fear of retribution, and you feel known for who you truly are.

Together, you and your love know how to weather the bumps in the road, and you learn from your shared difficulties as well. You've learned to talk your problems through, come to understandings, and learn from them. No one's ego is in charge in this kind of relationship. Your heart is instead.

If you know love like this, I'm sure you would agree it is one of life's most profound essentials. And if you haven't, I'm here to say it's possible—and the heart of joy. It took me a large chunk of my adult life and a whole lot of learning to find such a relationship, but my second marriage has been nothing short of miraculous.

The key, surprisingly, has been making myself the priority, returning to self-care, and allowing that love to come find me, but only when the time was right. It took me two years to recover from a difficult relationship before I could date again.

By then, I'd learned what works for me and what doesn't. I knew exactly the kind of person I wanted to be with, and I set my bar high enough to meet my needs. Then I chose my mate accordingly.

While it's not in the scope of this book to advise on how to create or maintain such a relationship, know there are a lot of experts out there who are eager to advise you. For me, it was critical to find a dating coach when I was ready. I'd had too many tough relationships and unhealthy patterns in my past to fully trust my own radar.

My coach pointed out difficult realities I didn't want to see as I went out on a string of first dates, and she urged restraint at all the right times. Then, when I found my true love, she sent me off with her blessing. It was exactly the guidance I needed.

So now let me ask you a question. What shape is your love life in?

Are you happy in the knowledge that at least one person in this life totally, truly knows you, cares about you, and provides the intimate comfort and support you need? Or is love a dramatic racetrack full of dangerous drivers, warning flags, and hazards ahead?

Or perhaps love is just not happening, and you like it that way. Do you know in your heart you need to be alone at this time? Or do you shy away from love because you fear there's no point and you'll just get hurt again?

Are you in a long-term relationship that has lost its spark? Are you longing for something you just can't seem to find? Do repairs or changes need to be made? Does the relationship actually need to end?

More importantly, would renewed or new love bring you back to yourself in a powerful way if you would just allow it in?

On the other hand, if you lost a love relationship recently through a divorce, a breakup, or a death, you may be in a fertile place of healing right now, which is best not disturbed.

It can take years after a nasty divorce or the death of a loved one to recover enough to begin a new relationship. If that's where you're at, enjoy your time alone and feel free to do the journaling exercise on page 160, just answer the last question, or skip the exercise altogether, as you wish. If you're in a relationship, open to one, or actively dating, read on.

Here is the perfect moment to be honest with yourself, no matter what the state of your love life. Close your eyes, take three long, slow relaxing breaths, and do some journaling on the following questions.

You may even want to close the door, pour yourself a cup of tea or a glass of wine, and let the thoughts flow.

*Boundaries are important...
Set boundaries on love. There is no
limit to the amount of love you can
give or receive, but you can limit
who you give and receive to.*

—TEAL'S JOURNAL, SEPTEMBER 11, 2011

Good Questions to Ask
Yourself about Love

Fill this out if you are in a committed relationship.

What do you love about your relationship?

What bothers you about your relationship?

What would you consider changing?

What need is not being fulfilled at present?

What needs are being abundantly fulfilled?

What are you craving in this relationship?

What are you grateful for in this relationship?

Who are you in this relationship?

Who would you like to be?

Where is the joy in being with this person?

What support do you need that you're not currently getting?

What requests do you need to make?

List five to ten adjectives that describe your current relationship.

Fill this out if you are actively dating or looking for love.

Are you clear on what you want?

Are you looking for committed love or are you just available for fun dates right now?

Are you finding plenty of possible candidates?

Think about your dating history. Are there any patterns?

Are you a serial dater who is never satisfied?

Do you need more support with this process?

List five to ten adjectives that describe your ideal relationship.

Fill this out if you are single and not actively pursuing love right now.

If you could change anything about your life right now, what would it be?

Do you see yourself sharing your life with someone right now?

If not, why not?

What would love bring to your life?

How might love complicate your life?

What would your love bring to someone else's life?

Name five activities you prefer to do alone.

List five activities you prefer to do with someone you love.

What do you miss most about being in a love relationship?

What have you learned by being single?

What is easier about being single?

What's more difficult about being single?

Do you have a pattern of avoiding relationships?

List five to ten adjectives that describe your current state of being single.

If you answered these journaling questions, take what you have learned to heart. This is your chance to tell yourself the truth.

What has this process taught you about you and your relationship with love?

Build This into Your Life

So what can you do to take what you've learned and increase your serenity around love and relationships?

What are three actions you can take within a week regarding love?

1. ....
2. ....
3. ....

What are three actions you can take within a month regarding love?

1. ....
2. ....
3. ....

Good clarity! Now, determine when you will take these actions. Are there any you can do right now? Perhaps a phone call you can make or a text you can send?

Put more extensive items, like conversations, on your calendar now. And remember, you need this as much as the other person does.

You really do.

If you find yourself wavering or resisting this, drop by our Self-Care Group for Extremely Busy Women on Facebook and post your goals or actions you plan to take. And ask for the support you need. We are there for you.

twenty-six
essential #3:
friends and family
you can count on

....

We all need someone to pour our hearts out to, just as we need someone to spend a hilarious Saturday night with. Friends are an invaluable, precious part of life, and family are...well...family. Not only are they the people you'd do anything for, they can drive you straight up the wall. Yet they know you—and possibly love you—like no one else.

Ideally, your family and friends are a great source of wisdom, comfort, and joy. They are people you can freely, happily talk to and get support from when needed. Yet if you're like some of us, there are gaps in the system.

You have true friends for whom you would give anything. They are always there, no matter what, and you have been through the best and the worst together. You may even have a "chosen family," as opposed to your biological family, whom you prefer to treat as your closest kin.

But sometimes there are friends and family members who suck the life out of you. They are takers rather than givers, and they always seem to be having some sort of emergency or demand. They challenge you, but not in a good way.

You leave your time with them feeling slightly bruised, yet you keep going back for more, even though each time, you tell yourself this is the last time.

If this reminds you of someone close to you, your adrenal glands may be asking you to reconsider your actions. In fact, I know they are.

True friends are the ones who soothe and comfort you and whom you, in turn, love to soothe and comfort. These are the old souls who've traveled the path alongside you again and again, and their presence is critical to your life.

Yet I maintain the takers are old souls you've traveled with as well, only their purpose is not to soothe and comfort this time around. Rather, it's to wake you up so you will finally put your foot down and set a limit. And they can be just as important as the soothing, comforting friends we love to hang with. Because these folks are actually our teachers as well.

Each time you tell your own personal truth, you feed your soul, and that is a very high act of self-care indeed. Here's an example from my own life.

I once had a housemate who was funny and charming and knew no boundaries. The day I arrived, she rearranged "my" shelf in the kitchen after I carefully moved in all my food. But I said nothing. Instead, I decided the blaring warning sirens going off in my head were wrong. I told myself that she was just trying to help.

Over the months that followed, this housemate would park in my carefully negotiated parking place, cajole me repeatedly about extending my lease in her space, and barrel through my door when I needed to have a good cry by myself. I let her, of course, because I didn't know how to set any limits.

Instead, I kept playing out an old pattern of silence, despite my discomfort.

And yet, at the same time, we became fast friends. We comforted each other through our recent losses with copious replays of *Downton Abbey*, red wine, and cheesecake. We made each other laugh. And we both understood that nobody is perfect.

Still, much as I appreciated this friend, I never felt entirely safe in her home. Even though I finally gave in and extended my lease, I ultimately decided to move out early, despite the upset I knew this would cause. But I didn't care at this point. I simply had to go. It was what my heart was asking for.

Our final encounter was raw and furious as I said what was on my mind instead of remaining silent. It was not okay to live with someone who kept blowing past my boundaries. I realized that, and I needed to speak up about it. A firestorm followed, but I got out of there with my wits still intact.

My housemate was undoubtedly an important teacher, for she provided me with a critical wake-up call. Suddenly, I realized her problems were not my problems, and I had healing of my own to do.

I saw how important listening to myself was and even sharing my own anger where appropriate. Even if she didn't like it.

I understood that in the end we—just us, our hearts and our souls—are really all we've got. Yes, we have family, friends, and true loves, but ultimately, we need to stand in our own truth. This is a lesson I've continued to carry with me and apply in a number of different ways in my life.

We need to ask for what we need and stick up for our own values. That is our responsibility as people on this planet, pure and simple. It is also our greatest gift.

Ask yourself this: is there someone you've been withholding important things from? This is the essence of your intimacy with the world. You simply have to get in the habit of sharing your truth, even when it means making a vulnerable apology or request.

This is what being a great friend or family to others is really all about. Not only do they have a deeper understanding of who you are, you provide the space for them to be vulnerable as well.

This is how those who are truly connected to you become closer and closer allies. And those who are simply takers drift away, as you set the limits your heart demands. This is how everything returns to balance in your world, and you find yourself more serene and more supported than ever.

All it takes is the courage to show up, speak your truth, and let the chips fall where they may, even if it leaves a few people bothered or bruised as you walk away. Ultimately, you will have lived out your karma together.

May you do so with ease and grace.

····· T W E N T Y   M I N U T E S ·····

Who's Got Your Back?

Here is an exercise to help you explore the value of your relationships with friends and family. This is best done with an open mind, in the name of exploration.

Begin this exercise by taking several long, deep breaths, getting quiet for a moment, and relaxing.

Make a list of at least ten people you care most about in this world. Let your mind pop up names for the list, and stay open. Do not try to engineer the list with those you think *should* be there, but instead let the list write itself. Prepare to be surprised. If you can't come up with ten people, that's okay too. (You can count couples and groups you feel equally connected to as one on the list.) Decide why you care about them. What qualities do they add to your life?

Name	They Add

In doing this exercise, what do you notice? Are you surprised that a certain person is included in the list? Are you surprised that someone is not on the list?

Now make a list of anyone in your life who drains your energy. This would be people who generally leave you feeling scared, anxious, upset, frustrated, annoyed, angry, uncertain, or unsafe. Again, go with your gut here. Don't add anyone you think *should* be on the list or remove anyone who shouldn't. Give yourself enough time to really listen to your heart.

Beside each person you listed, add the feelings you have after each encounter with that person. Don't get into specific circumstances. Just stick to your gut feelings.

Name	Feeling They Leave You With

Are you surprised by what you learned?

Build This into Your Life

Now you can see more clearly the cost or reward of certain relationships in your life.

Take a moment to write down with whom you could share some love in the next few days. Then take a moment to reach out to them. This could be a quick email or a text telling them how much you love them. Or you could surprise them with a card or a bouquet of flowers. Or whatever your heart tells you to do.

Then drop by our Self-Care Group for Extremely Busy Women on Facebook and tell us what you did and why. That just spreads love and inspiration.

Now think about those people around whom you may need to exercise some caution. Is there a limit you need to set around anyone on this list? Is there a situation you frequently find yourself in that could be changed to better meet your needs?

On the other hand, is there some responsibility you need to take for your frustrated feelings with these people? Often, our resentment with others masks underlying, deeper frustration with ourselves. Is there a conversation you need to have with someone, whether it's a request or an apology that would simply take the pressure off? You know this is true when you feel uncomfortable just thinking about him or her.

Whom will you talk to and by when?

Who	When

Now go ahead and book that time in your calendar. And if you find yourself avoiding the task when the time comes, check in with your self-care buddy on this, before and after you have that chat.

twenty-seven
essential #4:
real vacations

....

Notice I wrote the word vacations, *as in lots of them.* Who would think such a thing is possible? But it is, my friend. It really is.

First, let's begin with why you need a vacation in the first place. Unless you just returned from one, I recommend you wrap your head around taking a proper vacation immediately.

The mere thought for a lot of us extremely busy women is "I can't! Who's going to X, Y, and Z!" or "What about the [kids, cats, etc.]?" We have a million reasons why we simply can't take time off right now. But next year, maybe...

Screw next year! Here's what avoiding a vacation is costing you right now. Women who only take vacations every six years are *eight times* more likely to develop heart disease or have a heart attack as those who take two vacations per year.*

- - - - - - - - - - - - - - - - - -

* Alina Tugend, "Take a Vacation, for Your Health's Sake," *New York Times*, June 8, 2008, https://www.nytimes.com/2008/06/08/business/worldbusiness/08iht-07 shortcuts.13547623.html.

Studies have found that not only do missed vacations impact your health and personal relationships, but you also become less productive as you continue to slog away without a break. CNN reports that taking vacations can improve your work productivity by 80 percent.*

Yet at the same time, we avoid vacations. A frightening 2016 study found that 54 percent of Americans ended the prior year without using all their vacation days. And nearly 59 percent of millennial workers feel "vacation shamed" for taking time off at work.†

Which means all those millions of workers are now more vulnerable to burnout, cardiovascular disease, and who knows what else, and they are also less creative, productive, and happy than they could be. The economy suffers as well. It's been calculated that due to missed vacation time, $236 billion go unspent. If that vacation-deprived 54 percent would just take one more day away per year, they'd contribute another $33 billion to the U.S. economy.‡

It's remarkable just how far down into your psyche a good vacation reaches. Time off not only soothes your tired body, it also refreshes your mind, bolsters your spirits, and reminds you of all the good in life.

---

* Chuck Thompson, "Americans Taking Fewest Vacation Days in Four Decades," CNN, October 23, 2014, https://www.cnn.com/travel/article/u-s-workers-vacation-time /index.html.

† Neil Howe, "Why America's Overstressed Workers Won't Take a Break," Forbes, June 30, 2017, https://www.forbes.com/sites/neilhowe/2017/06/30/why-americas-over stressed-workers-wont-take-a-break/#345faf73491f.

‡ Ozgur Tore, "Unused Vacation Time Costs the U.S. Economy $236 Billion," FTN News, May 29, 2017, https://ftnnews.com/tours/32380-unused-vacation-days-cost -the-u-s-economy-236-billion.

This means you come back to work refreshed, renewed, and ready to kick proverbial butt.

Now here's the thing I love most. Three-day vacations, either on the weekend or in the middle of the week, can do the trick nicely. Manhattan-based psychotherapist and author Jonathan Alpert says that taking three days off can be as beneficial for your psyche as taking off an entire week.[§]

However, it's good to mix in some longer vacations as well if you can. Researchers have also noticed that most vacations peak and crest in overall happiness around the eight-day mark, which is good news if you happen to have fourteen days of paid vacation per year.[¶] This means if you plan strategically, you can take three eight-day vacations in a year. And that is some seriously good self-care.

Where should you go on vacation, especially if you're not feeling flush enough to take three separate vacations each year? Staycations are always an option. But for God's sake, stay out of the work zone! And don't even think of doing this if you work from home or even near your home. Instead, really get out and explore your local area like a tourist. Or, ideally, get out of town.

See if you can stay at a friend's cabin in the woods or explore arranging a house swap using websites like HomeExchange.com.

----

§   Stacey Leasca, "Getting Away for a 3-Day Weekend Could Make You Happier Than a Long Vacation," *Travel + Leisure*, September 20, 2018, https://www.traveland leisure.com/travel-tips/three-day-weekend-trips-better-than-longer-vacation.

¶   Sima Shakeri, "8 Days Is the Perfect Vacation Length, Study Says," *Huffington Post*, September 15, 2017, https://www.huffingtonpost.ca/2017/09/15/8-days-is-the-perfect -vacation-length-study-says_a_23211082/.

Visiting relatives or old friends is an option as well, unless you tend to come back feeling depressed or annoyed from such visits.

Be honest with yourself about what you really need and whom you want to be around.

And then ask your body. What kind of environment is your body actively craving? Seaside? Complete change of scenery? Deep foreign culture immersion? An everything-done-for-you cruise or resort? If you ask, the answer will come up. And it just might be surprising, so stay open. Again, if you think you're unlikely to ever get around to taking that vacation, please go back and read the beginning of this chapter. Then ask yourself how long you would like to live.

Above all, don't let anyone talk you out of your much-deserved vacation. Your office, team, staff, and colleagues really can get along without you for a while.

Why not begin planning your next vacation now with the following exercise?

Build This into Your Life

In order to afford my vacations, I find it helpful to save a certain amount of money each month and place it in a specifically labeled vacation savings account. I enjoy watching it grow month by month. Then it's a great feeling to go vacation shopping with the money in hand. If you think you're going to have trouble actually saving for a vacation, let the auto transfer service at your bank handle the savings for you each month. Even $50 a month is a start. Just start somewhere.

As you accumulate those savings, set up both paper files and a digital file folder on your computer labeled Vacation Ideas. Fill that file with clippings from articles, pictures of things that look fun, and links to good travel stories, fun-sounding tours, and more.

Keep track of books on certain locations as well, including novels. Authors as diverse as Mark Twain and Jack Kerouac have written inspiring accounts of their travels that just make you want to see more and more. Take a look in your local library as well as at online booksellers for books on locations that appeal.

Don't know where you want to go? This is where travel agents can help, as well as discount travel brokers such as Costco Travel. Google search for terms like "vacation packages" to any destination with the year you'd like to travel, and you'll find rich resources as well.

Are you worried you'll be stuck alone in a foreign place with no local contacts? Don't forget about Airbnb, which has affordable rooms in people's houses for rent. Whether you rent an entire home or apartment or just a room, you will indeed have a local connection who can be useful for all manner of things.

Another fun option is home exchange, in which you trade homes, cars, and sometimes even pets with someone else, potentially on the other side of the world. You may find yourself with a free place to stay in Hawaii, Barcelona, Paris, or the moors of England. A good source for home exchanges is HomeExchange (homeexchange.com), though there are many to choose from.

····· TWENTY MINUTES ·····

Instant Vacation Planner

When's the last time you took a vacation? How long was it?

On a scale of 1 to 10, 10 being incredibly excellent, how would you rate that vacation?

What really worked about that getaway?

What didn't work about it so much?

**What did you learn, if anything,
from your last vacation?**

Now close your eyes and tune into your body. Take five deep, slow breaths, and ask yourself where you'd like to go on a vacation. Allow the vision to unfold in your mind. Do not stop to consider the logistics of this vacation or any related details.

Instead, focus on what you want and need, right here and right now.

Now that you've begun to get a little information, open your eyes and begin journaling on these questions:

Is this a vacation to a place you know and love or somewhere completely different?

Are you going alone or taking a good friend?

Is there some kind of activity, experience, or outing you want to be sure to include?

What else have you been
craving from a vacation?

What is one thing you've always
wanted to do on a vacation?

When would you like to go?

How long would you like your vacation to be?

Okay, now that you have your starter vision for a vacation, do not allow yourself to back down, cave in, or run away. Instead, arrange for some time off—even if it means getting out of your comfort zone.

If you're lousy at making plans, buying tickets, and such, or if you truly don't have time, hire a travel agent. The cost will be minimal, and the support will be real. Or get a travel buddy to join you. Get help and do not do this alone.

I promise you, you will be seriously thankful you took your vacation. May this be the start of many more holidays to come.

····· FIFTEEN MINUTES ·····

Do You Need a Retreat?

Sometimes a vacation isn't exactly what we need. Instead, we just need to escape completely from the world for a while. We need to climb into our own little bubble and relax in an entirely new way. We might even need to tangle with big life issues or pending transitions, so we need a good place to rest and think.

A retreat is a getaway to a place where you can be either entirely alone or surrounded by enough creature comforts (i.e., hot springs, nature walks, yoga classes, massages, etc.) to do a reboot of your central nervous system. Retreat centers tend to be places that do not allow alcohol, and some even have a spiritual theme or require silence. Unlike resorts, they are designed to help you return to complete mental and physical health.

On the other hand, you may choose to take a tent and go into the woods for your retreat. To find the perfect place to take your retreat, scan the online options and ask your body which ones feel right. She'll help you get there.

This questionnaire will help you sort out whether a vacation or an actual retreat is what is needed next.

The best word I could use right now to describe myself is

a. On fire!

b. Content

c. Clouded and distracted

d. Downright cranky or depressed

e. Stressed out and completely overwhelmed

I would describe my energy as

a. Abundant

b. Pretty good

c. Seeking a new level but not there yet

d. Frazzled

e. Exhausted

When I think about my current level of self-care, I

a. Feel happy and proud

b. Am a little worried

c. Know it's wrong, but I can't stop and change it

d. Don't like to think about it

e. Feel sad and frustrated, even angry

My health is

a. Excellent

b. A work in progress

c. Currently neglected, but I'll get to it...maybe

d. A problem I know I need to solve

e. Chronically or seriously ill

In terms of life, do I have big decisions or transitions to make?

a. Nope. I'm on an even keel.

b. Things are starting to shift, but not quite yet.

c. I feel dread as I think about them.

d. Yes, and I'm not sure how to move forward.

e. I am in crisis mode and need help.

The last time I was in a truly quiet, nurturing place was

a. In the last three months

b. In the last year

c. In the last two years

d. Five to seven years ago

e. Not in recent memory

The idea of being on retreat

    a.   Doesn't feel super relevant

    b.   Is mildly interesting

    c.   Sounds good and I may be ready

    d.   Relaxes my whole system just reading this

    e.   Makes me realize I NEED TO GO!

When it comes to retreats, I typically

    a.   Do them on a regular basis, and I benefit every time

    b.   Have gone on some and want more

    c.   Know I need a retreat but I'm not sure how to make it happen

    d.   Think I don't deserve a retreat

    e.   Avoid them. Going on one seems impossible.

If someone offered me a few days or even a week of simply resting and being cared for, I would

    a.   Thank them very much and say yes!

    b.   Accept...with a little worry about my responsibilities

    c.   Maybe go, but only if it was really easy to get away

    d.   Cry from gratitude

    e.   Insist I couldn't go (because I couldn't take the time off)

Now take a moment to review your answers and see how they stack up with the following suggested guidelines.

If you had:

► **Mostly a's:** You are becoming a self-care aficionado! You know the benefit of a great retreat, and you have manifested many in your life. Do you need a retreat now? Close your eyes and see what answer swims up to the surface. You know.

► **Mostly b's:** You're definitely making a shift. A retreat is a good choice if it supports this transition you are in right now. And why wouldn't it? Do you long for a retreat in your heart?

► **Mostly c's:** In your heart of hearts, you know there is work to do in your self-care. This is work that could be well supported by a retreat. Be honest with yourself. Has the time finally come?

► **Mostly d's:** If you're someone who struggles with self-care, perhaps it's time to give yourself permission to let go and rest. Close your eyes and rest for just a minute. Has your need for a retreat gotten to critical yet? Can you finally let go?

► **Mostly e's:** Is it time to take everything apart and start anew? That's the value of a total break in the routine. A retreat can be a great idea if this falling apart is fully supported. For instance, you might not want a solo retreat, but one with staff, teachers, helpers, or even therapists who will guide you. Above all, remember *you* are your most important priority. Don't hesitate to take action now.

Want help creating your own self-care retreat? Learn how to set up your own retreat at my resource library at suzannefalter.com /freeresources. Just click on "Planning Your Own Self-Care Retreat."

Your body is a temple. Your mind is a fountain. Treat them as such, and you will be healed.

—TEAL'S JOURNAL, SEPTEMBER 17, 2011

twenty-eight
essential #5:
great energy

. . . .

How's your energy? Do you wake up in the morning refreshed and ready to go? Or is it a long haul to the coffee maker?

Do you even remember what it was like to spring out of bed as a carefree kid in the mornings? Because once, you actually had that boundless energy. If you play your cards right, you can experience the zing in life again. You may simply need to develop some new habits.

Along with getting adequate sleep, the key is in maintaining your body's systems through diet and exercise. There really is no other way around it. What you put in greatly affects what you get back, from your adrenal function to your blood pressure.

Consume too much sugar or carbs and you basically caramelize the delicate coating of your nerves. Too much alcohol can ruin your sleep and deplete your motor coordination and even your ability to think clearly. Too much pasta, potatoes, or rice for dinner and you can wake up drenched in sweat. Then there's caffeine, Ben & Jerry's, and the evil potato chip. Energy saboteurs surround us.

We're not talking weight here. We're just talking energy, because that's what us extremely busy women need, right? Still, the sad truth prevails. You can work all you want, but if you overload your system with too much of the stuff that doesn't serve it, it will stop serving you.

And that's before you get to complicating factors like injuries, aging, stress, chronic diseases, and menopause.

We all know about the merits of eating a healthier diet, so I won't get into that here. Suffice it to say that you want ample protein, fiber, greens, and veggies. And it's best to consume fewer carbs and reduce or cut out sugar and alcohol to maximize your energy.

Resources abound online that can guide you toward a better diet, including green smoothie apps and endless lists of ways to eat healthy.

The bigger issue, perhaps, is exercise.

Believe me, I understand. Exercise for some of us is a bear, plain and simple. We know we're supposed to do it. And yet...

It's so very easy to decide that we simply don't have time.

Did you know that regular moderate exercise can substantially increase your mojo? We're only talking *moderate* exercise here. You don't even have to work up a big sweat. Walking, for instance, is just fine.

A study at the University of Georgia found that just three twenty-minute sessions of walking per week helped a group of non-exercisers increase their energy by 20 percent. And 65 percent of them reported less general fatigue at the end of six weeks.*

Tim Puetz, a researcher involved in the study noted, "Too often we believe a quick workout will leave us worn out—especially when we are already feeling fatigued. However, we have shown that regular exercise can actually go a long way in increasing feelings of energy—particularly in sedentary individuals."

The U.S. Department of Health and Human Services says we need a total of 150 minutes of moderate exercise per week. This alone will give us 85 percent of the benefits we need. Or, if we have less time, seventy-five minutes of vigorous exercise per week will also do the trick.† That's only four twenty-minute workouts. Ideally, strength training can be added twice a week as well.

If you think you have no time to work out, consider this. The *Journal of American Medicine* reports that you can stockpile exercise into one long exercise per week. This means going for the entire 150 minutes in a single bike ride, hike, or workout once a week, instead of five thirty-minute rides or walks.‡ It may take a while to get through it and be pretty darn tiring.

----

*   Sam Fahmy, "Low Intensity Exercise Reduces Fatigue Symptoms by 65 Percent, Study Finds," *UGA Today*, February 28, 2008, https://news.uga.edu/low-intensity-exercise-reduces-fatigue-symptoms-by-65-percent-study-finds/.

†   President's Council on Sports, Fitness & Nutrition, "Physical Activity Guidelines for Americans," https://www.hhs.gov/fitness/be-active/physical-activity-guidelines-for-americans/index.html.

‡   Marissa Higgins, "How Many Times a Week Should You Work Out? Once Might Be Enough But There's a Catch," *Bustle*, January 11, 2017, https://www.bustle.com/p/how-many-times-a-week-should-you-work-out-once-might-be-enough-but-theres-a-catch-29689.

Still, as long as it gets you out and exercising, do what works.

If you're like many of us, a regular exercise routine makes sense, but it is just plain elusive. Then the question must be asked: how can you make working out fun for yourself? What's the missing piece that will connect your good intentions with taking action?

Often, it's hard to keep a date with ourselves. That's when a personal trainer or an exercise buddy is helpful. Arrange to meet someone at the gym who will notice your presence if you don't show up. If you find you keep cancelling gym dates, then it's time to have a little talk with yourself.

What are you getting out of avoiding exercise? I ask because if this is a continued problem, you are using resistance to avoid some other, possibly larger issue.

Are you nervous about being seen in form-fitting gym clothing or, worse, naked in the locker room? Or are you dreading the potential pain of those first rusty workouts? Do you consider yourself to be not great at exercise, or are you afraid of an old injury flaring up? (See the journaling questions beginning on page 198 to dig into these matters more completely.)

All this can be handled with clarity, the right mindset, and some good workarounds. Find a dressing booth or a bathroom stall to change in if need be. And skip the form-fitting gym clothing if that's an issue. Start out in good old baggy sweats. Open your mind to trying something you've never done before, like African dance, Zumba, Pilates, or playing tennis.

And yes, if you're afraid of potential pain or injury, check in with your doctor before beginning any exercise program.

The key is to get yourself to begin and then to make exercise a regular, healthy habit in your life.

Does it seem impossible? Consider this. What if a life well lived wasn't about the struggle to achieve goals but setting up a series of self-care habits that become as automatic as rising, sleeping, and brushing your teeth? (More on this later.) For now, consider the possibility that exercise can also become a healthy habit in your life.

It's just a matter of establishing habits that make you a priority, no matter what.

So why not try experimenting with a few walks or gentle workouts for starters? Give this project no less than two months to establish itself. Then stop and reassess. Is the exercise plan you chose working for you? Or is there some better way to go about it? Is it fun enough? Does it feel good enough to be sustainable?

If you don't have a gym, then do some shopping around. Choose a place near enough to your home or workplace that you'll actually go there. Make sure it has what you want, whether that be early morning yoga classes or a great outdoor pool.

Remember, you're choosing a sanctuary here. This gym or exercise studio really must be a place where you come back to yourself every time you go there. It's that important.

If you're more of an outdoor exerciser, figure out what that option might look like. Is there a beloved park nearby or hiking trails you haven't yet discovered? Is riding a bike to work a reasonable option? Or riding it somewhere else, like on specific bike trails? Consider doing something you haven't done before or perhaps for a long time. (One more reminder: what would be *fun*?)

Now, about that sticky issue of accountability. Will you actually show up and *do* the exercise?

If you have a competitive instinct, try getting into a program at your gym that tracks your progress and rewards accomplishments. Or consider using the stickK app, which uses financial incentives to lure you into completing the goals you set for yourself. If you don't keep your promises, you must pay $50 to either a designated charity or a friend. Or even a foe, if that will keep you committed.

Some gyms offer computer-based programs, like ActivTrax, that generate and track individualized printed or app-based workouts for you. (Ask your gym's administrators if they have it.) For me, ActivTrax has been a godsend because each workout is different, and variety is what keeps me motivated.

There are apps to guide workouts of all kinds, from walking to yoga. Even the Weight Watchers app, WW, has an audio program, Aaptiv, that coaches you through specific strength training and aerobic workouts.

····· FIFTEEN MINUTES ·····

Build More Exercise into Your Life

Some of us are gym avoiders. And we have our reasons, which we may or may not be aware of. If this applies to you, take a few moments with your journal to answer the following questions. See if anything dawns on you in the process.

How do you feel about working out?

If you haven't worked out recently, why?

**What's the best time of day
for you to work out?**

**If you don't have a gym, where would you
like it to be? What should it offer?**

**When you think about working
out, what would be fun?**

Complete the following sentence:
"I'd work out more, except..."

Stop, take a few breaths, and think about what you wrote for the last answer. Close your eyes and see if there's another, bigger reason beyond that one. Then answer the question again:

"I'd work out more, except..."

Now complete this sentence:
"When I don't work out, I..."

Now take a look at all your answers. Assuming you chose a location(s) for exercise and a best time, book a time when you can tour at least one gym. (Gyms usually allow you to work out for free as well, sometimes for repeated visits, so plan some workout time too.)

Book two slots for exercise on your schedule in the coming week. If you really don't have enough time for a gym, make it a run or walk right out your front door. Start small so you don't overwhelm your body.

Once you experiment a bit and find the right exercise combo for you, you can expand this into a regular slot on your calendar.

A final note: The use of music while exercising has been found to have far-reaching beneficial effects, helping you run and bike farther and even swim at a faster speed. A researcher at London's Brunel University calls music "a type of legal performance-enhancing drug."*

May I just add it's also a damn good distraction from any pain that comes up while you're working out, as well as being just plain more fun. Those podcasts you never get a chance to listen to are an excellent addition as well. (As ever, use extreme caution if working out near traffic while wearing headphones.)

A Word about Adrenal Fatigue

If you're like many women who have their foot on the gas a little too much, your adrenal glands could be exhausted. Doctors tend

---

* "Legal Doping—Training to Tunes," Brunel University, London, September 27, 2016, https://www.brunel.ac.uk/research/News-and-events/news/Legal-doping-%E2%80%93 -training-to-tunes.

to disregard adrenal fatigue as unsubstantiated and unproven, but naturopaths, some chiropractors, and other holistic medical practitioners take it quite seriously.

This is not the same thing as Addison's disease, which is a body's inability to produce the fight-or-flight hormone cortisol and occasionally the hormone aldosterone. Instead, adrenal fatigue results when the adrenal glands can't keep up with the onslaught of cortisol responses the typical hardworking woman has in a day.*

You know the fight-or-flight response. It's that tense, skin-crawling intensity that shoots up your spine when panic or anxiety sets in. Which it may over the copier paper being out, a police car pulling you over on the highway, or even a pressing deadline. Adrenal rushes seem to happen a *lot* in our world.

You may have adrenal fatigue if you wake up tired all the time, regardless of how much sleep you get. Body aches, skin discoloration, low blood pressure, and unexplained weight loss are among the symptoms. The cure has to do with slowing down, sleeping in, fortifying yourself with certain supplements, and removing sugar, excessive carbs, and caffeine from your diet.

The expert on this and the man who coined the phrase *adrenal fatigue* is Dr. James L. Wilson. You can take his handy test assessing

----

* "Adrenal Insufficiency (Addison's Disease)," Pituitary Network Association, https://pituitary.org/knowledge-base/disorders/adrenal-insufficiency-addison-s-disease; Todd B. Nippoldt, "Adrenal Fatigue: What Causes It?" Mayo Clinic, https://www.mayoclinic.org/diseases-conditions/addisons-disease/expert-answers/adrenal-fatigue/faq-20057906; "What Is Cortisol?" WebMD, https://www.webmd.com/a-to-z-guides/what-is-cortisol#1.

your adrenal state at adrenalfatigue.org. While adrenal fatigue is not always recognized by mainstream MDs, a good naturopath or chiropractor can help if you think this might be an issue.

Drink Water for More Energy

Up to 75 percent of all Americans are dehydrated, according to a University of Florida study.[†] (You know this is you if your urine is dark. If it's clear or nearly colorless, you are in good shape.)

The negative effects of dehydration, which include everything from weakness to dizziness, headaches, and hunger pangs, are bad enough. But a surprising fact is that drinking enough water—really enough water—can seriously boost your energy.

Why? Water makes up nearly 60 percent of the body's composition.[‡] When you are properly hydrated, your organs can function at their peak, requiring less of your overall energy. Even mild dehydration can cause your body's systems to slow down, leaving you feeling sluggish.

Average healthy adults need to drink the equivalent of around three quarts of liquid per day, according to the Mayo Clinic.[§] That

- - - - - - - - - - - - - - - - -

[†] Dahlia Ghabour, "Studies Show Most Americans Are Dehydrated," April 14, 2015, in *Health in a Heartbeat*, podcast, MP3 audio, 2:00, https://podcasts.ufhealth.org /studies-show-most-americans-are-dehydrated/.

[‡] "The Water in You," USGS Water Science School, https://water.usgs.gov/edu /propertyyou.html.

[§] "Water: How Much Should You Drink Every Day?" Mayo Clinic, September 6, 2017, https://www.mayoclinic.org/healthy-lifestyle/nutrition-and-healthy-eating/in-depth /water/art-20044256.

number might need to be higher if some of those drinks are caffein-ated or you're pregnant, breastfeeding, or sweating heavily.

Don't wait until you are thirsty to drink water, because by then, you will already be slightly dehydrated. Instead, carry a water bottle with you and keep hydrating all day long. You can even use an accountability app to keep you on target with this.

A final tip: add flavor notes to your water intake. This can really help you avoid energy-killing choices like juices, coffee, sodas, and sugary drinks. My personal favorites include a squeeze of blood orange, a few raspberries or a strawberry, and a slice of cucumber.

Build More Nutrition into Your Life

Here are some assorted pro-energy ideas that will help you avoid sugar and carbs and generally consume a healthier diet.

Each morning, fill a quart-sized mason jar with water and some kind of appealing flavor agent. A few strawberries or a squeeze of lemon and a sprig of mint make your water truly refresh-ing. Drink that water while you're commuting to work or before you leave the house. Then repeat at lunchtime, and fill up again later. By midafternoon, you will have drunk the recommended daily quota of ninety-six ounces of liquid. I can't stress the importance of flavor elements. They will help retrain your palate if you're used to sugary sodas and juices. Blood orange slices are fun too.

Cut back on alcohol with a no-sugar mocktail. When you set out to wean yourself off of, say, the nightly beer or glass of wine, find a healthy substitute that's still delightful. I like a soda called Spindrift, which is nothing more than sparking water with real squeezed fruit in seven flavors from mango orange to cucumber. And they are seriously delicious with virtually no sweetener or artificial ingredients (spindriftfresh.com). I keep them in the refrigerator, and whenever I get a craving, I open one up, pour it in a pretty wine glass, and thoroughly enjoy it. Spindrift has become my preferred evening mocktail.

Cut back on sugar with satisfying substitutes. This requires figuring out what you really like that happens to be healthy. For me, it's a handful of fresh raspberries or maybe a tablespoon of coconut butter. (This is the pulp of the coconut, pureed into a butter like peanut butter.) Unsweetened carob chips work wonders as well. Then get in the habit of reaching for them instead of the old sugar-filled standby when cravings hit. As your energy improves and your cravings subside, you will ultimately find them more satisfying.

Another favorite treat is "car candy." I combine carob chips, raisins, nuts, pumpkin seeds, and toasted coconut flakes in a bag and stash it in my glove compartment. Give them a day or two to melt and coagulate while the car is parked in the sun. Then take them out at a cooler moment, and you've got a seriously delicious candy with no chocolate, no sugar. Nothing but the good stuff.

Discover great carb alternatives for dinner. Just recently, I made a gorgeous pasta sauce—lots of grass-fed beef, some lovely tomatoes, a little red wine, fresh mushrooms. It was so delicious! And instead of putting it on pasta, I spooned it over steamed broccoli and added a bit of grated Parmesan on top. The same can be served on steamed cauliflower or even cauliflower that has been turned into a sort of rice in the food processor. Spiralized zucchini ("zoodles"), winter squash, and many other low-carb alternatives can replace the carb-rich staples like pasta, bread, and rice. You just have to give them a try.

Get sugar, booze, and processed foods out of your house. If you're serious about giving your adrenals a rest and committing to a high-energy, low-carb diet, the first things that have to go are the juices, sodas, beers, wine, and margarita mix. Likewise for the stashes of cookies, ice cream, chocolate bars, and other desserts. At least start there. Then gradually wean yourself off the other snack kingdom—the chips, pretzels, crackers, and salty treats that add a lot of unnecessary carbohydrates as well. Give yourself a month to withdraw from your old comfort foods while busily trying all kinds of substitutes.

Do the same thing for your desk at work. Remove all the junk food, and either throw it out or give it away. Then resupply yourself with healthier items from the raw food section of your grocery store or bags of nuts and dried fruit from the bulk section. (Avoid premixed packages of trail mix that tend to have chocolate in them. Also, given the sugar content in dried fruit, enjoy these in moderation.) A few cans of flavored water will work here as well.

Grow fresh herbs. Pots of spearmint and stevia on a sunny windowsill can be valuable helpers in your new quest to eat healthy and avoid sugar. Stevia, a natural sweetener, is forty times sweeter than sugar, has no calories, and does not affect your blood sugar. Chop it up and throw it on your morning oatmeal if you miss sugar, or chew a bit after dinner if you're craving sweets. Mint, meanwhile, is the perfect flavoring for so many things, beginning with your daily jars of water.

Discover the power of the smoothie. One of my greatest discoveries in the quest to eat more healthy food is the superfood smoothie. Julie Morris's cookbook, *Superfood Smoothies*, was life-altering for me. Not only is every single smoothie in this book mind-blowingly delicious, the recipes are low sugar, low carb, and great natural energy enhancers. I will note that superfoods are expensive, so I didn't use them all the time. But when I did, the smoothies were even better! These make a terrific dessert substitute as well.

Your body is a temple. Stay away from harsh chemicals, toxins, and white sugar. Be organic, honor your body, exercise, use it, and let it know you believe it is a temple.

—TEAL'S JOURNAL, AUGUST 9, 2011

twenty-nine
essential #6:
honest-to-god fun

....

I'm not going to get all long-winded about one of the most critical life forces we know. Joy is essential to a life well lived. Yet at the same time, most of us could use the reminder to go out and have a little fun. Especially if we're mired in busyness most of the time.

Dr. Stuart Brown, head of the National Institute of Play (yes, this really exists), has concluded that fun is essential to life. Neurologically speaking, playing games and doing puzzles help maintain memory and thinking skills. Playing is even a critical way for adults to connect and has been proven in studies to keep relationships healthy.

As Dr. Brown puts it, "What you begin to see when there's major play deprivation in an otherwise competent adult is that they're not much fun to be around... The perseverance and joy in work is lessened and life is much more laborious."*

Furthermore, seemingly pointless, relaxed activities like doing jigsaw puzzles, doodling, and listening to music have been found to release dopamine in the brain. This chemical is largely responsible for your feelings of pleasure and tends to be reduced when excess stress hormones are present. Coloring, on the other hand, calms the amygdala, our fight-or-flight center of the brain, and that can have a mighty calming effect after a hard day.

So yes, fun and relaxation actually *are* totally necessary. And ironically, more fun will help you be more productive with your work.

Now if you haven't had much fun in a while, you may be out of ideas about what would bring the spark of joy back to your life. (Note: This is when a vacation is also advised.)

What follows is a journaling exercise that will help you get back in touch with the plain old joy in life.

---

* Sami Yenigun, "Play Doesn't End with Childhood; Why Adults Need Recess Too," *All Things Considered*, August 16, 2014, https://www.npr.org/sections/ed/2014/08/06/336360521/play-doesnt-end-with-childhood-why-adults-need-recess-too.

····· FIFTEEN MINUTES ·····

Your Idea of Fun Is...

Take a moment to do this when you can shut the door, relax, and go within.

Complete any statements that call to you. Take three centering breaths, then begin to write on the following prompts.

The last time I had fun was:

Here's why it was fun:

What I loved the most about that time was:

I needed this because:

What I notice about fun in my life is:

When I don't have enough fun, I tend to:

I know I need to have more fun when:

Some people I always have fun with are:

I love to go to:

I'd love to do:

Ten Ways I Could Relax and Have Fun

1.

2.

3.

4.

5.

6.

7.

8.

9.

10.

Build This into Your Life

Take a look at the Ten Ways I Could Relax and Have Fun list you made earlier. Scan the list lightly and pick three activities that speak to you. What could you do right now? What could you do in a week? What could you do within a month?

Now plan a fun break. Pick a window of at least two hours in your schedule when you can have a little me time. If it means you need to cancel a meeting and walk out of work early or take an extra-long lunch hour, do it. Do whatever it takes to arrange this time, even if it means hiring a babysitter or saying no to someone who expects a yes.

Reminder: You do this when you have to go to the doctor or dentist, right?

Note: You theoretically could use your usual television-viewing time for this slot. However, don't watch TV. Your usual stress relievers are not recommended for this exercise. Instead, choose something different that will truly refresh your nervous system.

Go ahead. You can do it. Block that time in. Then pick something from your list, and dig in and enjoy it. For me, this is jigsaw puzzling. The first time I put one together, I alternated between abject guilt ("How can I do something so pointless?") and delight.

Now I do jigsaw puzzles all the time, and the sky has not fallen, and my work has gotten done. With, I might add, far greater ease and far less suffering.

Once you have your fun break, ask yourself this. What did it cost you? And what was the benefit? If there was a cost, is there a way you could diminish it?

Make a point of having at least two or three fun breaks every week. Ideally, have one every day. They don't have to be two hours long. Or, on the other hand, they could be much longer!

essential *thirty* #7: your healing sanctuary

· · · · · · · · · · · · · ·

What's the interior of your car like?

If the mere thought calls to mind a back seat full of ditched soda bottles and a glove compartment stuffed with old Subway napkins, consider this. Your environment matters more than you may realize. According to Michael J. Formica, therapist and contributor to *Psychology Today*, the condition of your car is a reflection of the interior of your mind.[*]

Most of us go through life without a huge amount of thought about the space around us. Oh, we might hang a picture here and there or tidy up some now and then. But when you're busy, the state of your home is often an afterthought at best.

- - - - - - - - - - - - - - - - - -

[*] Michael J. Formica, "How the Environment We Create Is a Reflection of Our State of Mind," *Psychology Today*, https://www.psychologytoday.com/us/blog/enlightened-living/200807/how-the-environment-we-create-is-reflection-our-state-mind.

There are some of us who shudder at the mere thought of our bathrooms or our closets, and I understand. I've been there myself. Which is why I'm here to say that you deserve—and need—spaces around you that are clean, serene, well organized, and enjoyable to inhabit.

Not only will they add a nugget of joy to your life, they will soothe your jangled spirits and feed your energy. They will bring you back to yourself.

I learned this when I created a room for myself in my new partner's home. At first, the space was unremarkable. It was just another room with nice carpet and some decent blinds, but that was about it. Over the years, it had housed housemates, guests, and a TV, and it seemed like a forgotten space.

For the previous three years, I had lived in spare bedrooms in other people's homes while I grieved. The responsibility of a home seemed like more than I could handle. But I was ready, and I wanted something that was not only soothing but also beautiful and authentic. I sat in my new room with my unpacked boxes around me and imagined what I would like.

Immediately, I began to see it. Soon, the walls were being painted a deep salmon pink and the closet doors stained dark walnut. Soft overhead pin spots were installed where an altar would be created. I found a beautiful canopy bed frame for sale on Craigslist that was basically the bed of my dreams.

The length of ecru lace I'd purchased while I was grieving—for the home I knew I'd have again someday—soon hung from the bed's canopy. I even invested in some art restoration for a beloved but damaged painting to hang over my altar. When the room was complete, it was entirely transformed. And I adored it.

In this room, I've written books, retreated from the world, journaled my heart out, and had long, important chats with myself. And I've enjoyed every last minute of it. Here, I am surrounded by things I care about, from Kwan Yin, the goddess of compassion, on my altar to treasured pictures of Teal and my son, Luke, to the rocking chair my father rocked me in as a baby.

In my sanctuary, I can find the loose threads of my life and sew them up again. I can truly, deeply relax, knowing I am completely safe. And I can enjoy what I think is beautiful.

This is your opportunity too. For when someone works hard, doesn't she need a healing place to come back to? A place where her spirits can be soothed and her energy completely restored? This may be your home office or a bedroom of your own. Perhaps it's just a corner of a room that is entirely yours and yours alone. Maybe it's even your car.

Whatever the space, make sure you absolutely love it, that it soothes you, and that it has your personal stamp. You deserve no less.

By the same token, you may want to take a critical look at the office space you do most of your work in. Is it set up to serve you effectively? Does it inspire you to do your best, or is it overwhelming? Is there a way to make it more personal? More inspiring? More efficient?

I'm thinking of my friend Dale Marie, an exuberant banker who embodies joy and spirit. Not surprisingly, her corporate office space is loaded with her favorite color—purple. And I mean, there's a *lot* of purple.

While she couldn't paint the walls or change the official banker's furniture, Dale Marie has managed to add plenty of her own stamp: prints of lavender fields in France, teddy bears that wear purple party hats, a bejeweled purple water cup a client made for her, and multiple arrangements of purple flowers. Dale Marie positively glows in her office, and it serves her well at the same time, communicating who she is as a person well beyond her official role.

Take a look around the spaces you occupy the most as you move through your day. Do they delight and refresh you? Let your mind wander for a moment to those dark, cluttered corners of your life you've been tolerating for way too long.

If some of these spaces are making you cringe, there is no need to be ashamed. You *are* an extremely busy woman, right? No one says you have to be Martha Stewart on top of everything else. Instead, this is your opportunity to reboot.

You can, indeed, begin again. And yes, by all means, get help if that will make a big sort, a paint job, or a cleanup easier or more likely to happen. What you're going to notice when you are done improving your space is a *huge* improvement to your energy. You will have naturally upped your game by feeding yet another aspect of your self-care. Trust me on this. It's going to make a difference.

To ease this process, here's a questionnaire to help you sort through what works and what doesn't in your current environment.

····· T W E N T Y M I N U T E S ·····

Do You Truly Love Your Space?

Feel free to repeat this exercise for every space you occupy. As you answer the following questions, be sure to write down the very first thing you think of. Don't overthink it. You will gain clarity and a greater understanding of what's needed to enhance the good energy in your space.

Begin by sitting in the space you'd like to analyze and taking a good, long look at it.

Space being analyzed:

What do you use this space for?

On a scale of 1 to 10 (1 being abhor and 10 being adore), how do you feel about the space in general?

List five things you appreciate about the space.

List five things you would like to change.

How clean is the space on a scale of 1 to 10 (1 being filthy and 10 being spotless)?

Take another close look around. The specific areas that need cleaning are:

Does it need a paint job? If so, what color(s) would you prefer?

Does it need new flooring or carpet? What would you love underfoot?

How are the windows? Do they need
washing? New window treatments?

Does it need new upholstery, bed linens,
sofa pillows, or other fabric elements?

What shape are the closets in? When
you open them, how do you feel?

If you have a desk in the space, does it work
well for you? What would you change?

Do you need to add a standing desk, a more supportive
desk chair, or a more ergonomic computer setup?
(See the ergonomics discussion later in this chapter.)

If you have a filing or other storage system in the space, can you find what you need with ease?

If you could redo this space to be exactly what you want, what would that include?

Build This into Your Life

Taking on improving your living or working space can be daunting, so this work is best done by breaking it down project by project. If sorting and clearing out clutter is the issue, give yourself one small area to focus on each week, and give yourself plenty of time overall to get the job done.

Block in time on the calendar to research and hire help if needed. Then take a day or two off to do this organizing work if possible, or set aside a weekend. That helper can be a tremendous boon if you've been procrastinating about this for a long time. I promise this will be money and time well spent, because it will seriously renew you.

Give yourself plenty of time for renovations as well. The key is to get a clear vision of what you want to create, then take a few steps each week to move closer to your goal. By no means should you rush this process. It needs time to marinate and develop as you go.

Set aside some time on a weekend to clean out your car, really going through the dark corners and tossing out what must be tossed. Get some good music in your earbuds, and enjoy the process. You're giving this space some loving care, and you're going to be very gratified by the results.

Take note if you want to add a vanity plate or something else that might make the car more your own. After Teal's death, I turned my teal-colored car into a moving altar to her memory, adding small spiritual figurines and stickers. The console under the dash holds rose petals, and the license plate reads TEALSTR, for Tealster, her childhood nickname. The license plate holder carries one of her sayings: "Give fearlessly, and you shall never want."

Driving my memorial car has not only helped me feel more connected to Teal, it really expresses an important value about me and my life—honoring my daughter's memory.

A Word about Ergonomics and Your Office

How many hours do you spend at your desk each day? And how many of those hours do you sit?

This is a problem many of us are discovering as we hunch over our computers for hours every day. The result? A 64 percent increase in the likelihood of heart disease, an increased risk of obesity and cancer, and an average reduction of seven years in quality living according to sources including the National Cancer Institute.* You're especially at risk if you spend your evenings hunkered down in front of the TV.

Grim, I know. But there are solutions, like standing up and walking around. An out-of-the-chair break of five minutes every hour can seriously help, not to mention improve your mood.† Exercising

---

* Alice Park, "Sitting Can Increase Your Risk of Cancer Up to 66%," *Time*, June 16, 2014, http://time.com/2884953/sitting-can-increase-your-risk-of-cancer-by-up-to-66/.

† Georgina Bisby, "Sitting versus Standing—Where Do We Stand?" *Health & Safety Matters*, April 23, 2018, http://www.hsmsearch.com/page_662205.asp; Gretchen Reynolds, "Work. Walk 5 Minutes. Work," *New York Times*, December 28, 2016, https://www.nytimes.com/2016/12/28/well/move/work-walk-5-minutes-work.html.

a total of 2.5 hours per week can compensate nicely as well, according to a *Lancet* study. (That's only thirty minutes per day, five days a week.)* And then there's correct desk posture. Online articles abound on this topic, which is helpful, as this information continues to evolve rapidly.

Another solution is the standing desk, which can be an actual piece of furniture you purchase. Or it can be something you improvise, such as a large homemade box that sits on top of your desk, along with a computer elevator or elevation stand. These are sturdy metal and plastic stands that raise the level of your laptop or desktop computer so the screen is at eye level. I use one with my laptop and have noticed a huge improvement to my chronic neck and shoulder tension. Stretching also helps.

Then there's the issue of carpal tunnel syndrome from all that track pad use and endless keyboarding. According to the Bureau of Labor Statistics, work-related overuse injuries and repetitive stress injuries are among the most reported types of occupational illnesses.[†] And they've been on the rise.[‡]

You'll know this is you if your wrists, thumbs, or hands hurt

----

* Sarah Rense, "Just 2.5 Hours of Exercise Each Week Will Significantly Improve Your Life," *Esquire*, September 25, 2017, https://www.esquire.com/lifestyle/health/a1246 3686/minimum-exercise-hours-per-week/.

† "Musculoskeletal Disorders of the Upper Extremities," National Institute for Occupational Health and Safety, https://www.cdc.gov/niosh/docs/96–115 /diseas.html#Musculoskeletal%20Disorders%20of%20the%20Upper%20Extremities.

‡ Lisa Salmon, "Why Repetitive Strain Injury Is on the Rise," *Irish News*, January 27, 2016, http://www.irishnews.com/lifestyle/2016/01/27/news/rsi-becoming-increasingly -common-experts-warn-389271/.

while working or if you find you have unexplainable numbness, tingling, or pains shooting through your hands and arms. Begin by seeing your physician, of course, but also understand some basic changes to your desk setup may be required.

Fortunately, the marketplace has shifted to support a healthier workplace, and online information about this issue abounds. Know that an ergonomic office setup will seriously support your increased energy and zest as you move throughout your day.

thirty-one
essential #8: giving your brain a rest

....

In case you're wondering where we're going with these essentials, they are all ultimately pointed at one thing: your serenity.

By serenity, I mean a worry-free, smooth, clear state of mind devoid of drama and anxiety. Because when you have truly let go of your resistance and built a life that completely supports you, this is what you get.

Will there still be dramatic moments, bumps in the road, and lessons to learn? There certainly will. We get to learn and evolve with every difficulty we face and every choice we make. Meanwhile, the attaining of peace, the *ahhhhhh* feeling you get when in flow with your work or time off, is the refreshing sign that you are on the right track.

The goal is to become aware of and eventually to empty your mind of the following distractions. Remember that ease and serenity will be your reward if you can dial back or learn to work with this mental riffraff.

Gnashing your teeth. We all have people and situations that bug us, yet Buddha has some very good wisdom on this. In the parable known as "The Second Arrow," Buddha reminds a listener that we are unable to deflect the inevitable arrows of suffering in this life. But we have a choice about sending the second arrow in reaction to the first arrow.

For me, that second arrow is most punishing to myself as I try to compose the perfect angry retort or I rehash, for the fiftieth time, some way I think I was disrespected. The serene mind doesn't bother to engage in such petty scenarios. Instead, we go high and learn to ignore that particular impulse. Then the mental riffraff finally has a chance to disappear.

Each time we do that, the impulse to avoid the second arrow becomes stronger.

Endless worry and anxiety. What does worry get you? Stomach problems, insomnia, fatigue, and a gnawing sense that everything is not as it should be, for starters. Notably, it does not produce any actionable results. Instead, it trains us to turn to longing, wishing things were anything other than how they are, and endlessly marinating in our fears.

A reminder: this current reality you live in is your path, whether you like it or not. Best to go with it and then see what actually lies ahead. Undoubtedly, some good learning lies ahead. And as for your fears, you must learn to ask for help when necessary and then face down those demons, one at a time.

Shame. Shame's a beast, which is why so much has been written about it. For many of us, it feels embroidered onto our souls. We are at a loss on how, exactly, to avoid this black cloud of inner humiliation. To dissolve your shame, simply start where you are. If you notice you're full of shame, thank yourself for taking a moment to observe it. Then gently give yourself a few words of encouragement. On the other hand, if you would rather pretend it's not there, expect your shame to persist, chugging along as it always has.

The bottom line is that your shame cannot hurt you any more than it already has. For once the water is clouded, nothing but a thorough cleaning will right things. This might be the basis of a great retreat—an anti-shame cleanse, in which you celebrate and get to know more about you.

Smartphones and their apps. There is, of course, a time or place to pull out the apps. The problem is that the average amount of time an American spends on a smartphone is currently four to five hours per day. *That's a 100 percent increase in three years.* Yet the full effect of mobile technology on our brains is not fully understood. All we know is that more than twenty thousand people told the Bored and Brilliant Project, "It's messing with my productivity," "I feel addicted," and "It might actually be affecting my health."[*]

The excellent book *Bored and Brilliant* charts the path back to our natural creativity by helping readers wean themselves off of Smart phones and apps. Author Manoush Zomorodi, who created

----

[*]   Manoush Zomorodi, *Bored and Brilliant: How Spacing Out Can Unlock Your Most Productive and Creative Self* (New York: St. Martin's Press, 2017), 7.

this study, discovered that boredom is actually essential to brain health.

Downtime, away from all distractions, frees up our natural default setting, the official name for daydreaming. This is when wild, fun, creative thoughts bubble up and change the course of things, which is also where our natural brilliance lies.

So yes, you also need time to just be. Remarkable, isn't it? But then why should our innate design, with nothing added, be any less than perfect?

Why You Need Frequent Breaks from Work

Did you know that in order to work at your optimal pace and efficiency, you need frequent breaks? You'll know this is true if you spend inordinate amounts of time trying to get things done or you keep procrastinating endlessly on certain tasks.

A 2011 University of Illinois study found we lose our ability to focus and perform effectively after doing one task for too long, which is why frequent breaks are recommended for overall performance.[†] Turns out our brains, which are relatively small organs, use up an enormous amount of energy when concentrating on tasks. And they, too, need a rest.

[†] Diana Yates, "Brief Diversions Vastly Improve Focus, Researchers Find," *Illinois News Bureau*, February 8, 2011, https://news.illinois.edu/view/6367/205427.

What's a frequent break, and how long should it be? For starters, you are advised to get up from your desk, move around, and avoid all screens. Scrolling through Facebook or Twitter is not an effective break. The best idea, if possible, is to head outside, even if just for five minutes.

Walking in a green space is highly effective, which could be why 80 percent of the Apple campus in Northern California is reserved for green space, including an extensive orchard inside the ring formed by the building. Researchers from Heriot-Watt University call the effect of walking in a green space during breaks "meditative."*

Taking a coffee break, calling a friend, or chatting with fellow workers is also ideal, though avoid talking about work. That's not a break, right? The idea is to keep it light. Read a book, flip through a magazine, step outside to do some calming breathing, or do a little simple yoga stretching in the corner of your office instead. Even humming as you walk around can be an easeful break for your mind.

One friend I know kept an upright bass in his office, which he would pick up and start plucking when he felt mentally jammed. Another makes a point of keeping a book of poetry nearby, which she reads on a tranquil bench outside her office building.

Then there are those who like to work out at lunchtime, which kills several birds with one stone. Not only are you getting in

----

*   "Walk Through Green Space Could Help Put Brain in State of Meditation, Study
       Finds," *Huffington Post*, March 29, 2013, https://www.huffpost.com/entry/green
       -space-meditation-brain-walk-park_n_2964199.

much-needed exercise, which is a natural energy enhancer, but studies now show that moderate cardio can boost creativity and productivity for two hours afterward.

Some physiologists recommend taking a break every ninety minutes while working in order to synch with the body's own ultradian rhythm. Just as when we sleep, we naturally cycle through ninety-minute periods of alertness while awake. Other studies have found that a break every sixty minutes is more effective, as this is when we begin to lose focus.[†] Either way, when you feel your attention waning, walk away from the work.

The benefit is that you'll potentially return to your work with new insights, creative breakthroughs, or simply increased mojo.

Build This into Your Life

Breathe, my friend. Just breathe.

It helps me to have a small sign above my desk that says "Breathe."

Three to five slow, deep breaths can help a state of worry immediately dissolve.

Another thing that works well is the neuroplasticity exercise of talking to yourself. When we speak out loud and use our voices to talk down our feelings of anxiety in a firm, clear voice, we can gradually retrain our synapses to stop running down the usual, well-worn

---

[†]   Wanda Thibodeaux, "Why Working in 90-Minute Intervals Is Powerful for Your Body and Job, According to Science," *Inc.*, January 27, 2017, https://www.inc.com/wanda -thibodeaux/why-working-in-90-minute-intervals-is-powerful-for-your-body-and-job -according-t.html.

pathways. Basically, we're setting a limit with our brains. The same can be applied to feelings of shame as well.

And yes, you really do have to speak this aloud, with an appropriately firm tone.

The conversation with yourself would go something like this. "Hey, brain, quit making me feel anxious. It's a nice day out, my world is peaceful and serene, and there's nothing at all to be afraid of. I don't need these feelings. So quit doing this right now."

Also recommended by neuroplasticity therapists are quick, pungent sniffs of peppermint oil. The scent is so intense that it literally floods your brain, interrupting the usual neural pathways. Keep a vial handy in your desk. (You can buy it at health food stores.)

BONUS POINTS: Go to your nearest game or toy store, or shop online, and buy a fun-looking jigsaw puzzle. Then pull it out and put it together one night while you play some lovely music. Maybe even try this instead of the usual glass of chardonnay. Put it together with a friend or someone you love, and the effect is even more enhanced. If you feel guilty you're not doing something productive, just remember you are feeding your brain by stoking your dopamine. And you are building a relationship by simply relaxing over a puzzle with someone you want to spend time with. Not only will you recover, you'll have a much calmer, better day tomorrow.

You have so much to offer when you aren't worrying. Breathe away your worries and focus on the fire burning inside of you. Choose to only see the good in people and give positive answers and solutions. Love and be yourself!

—TEAL'S JOURNAL, SEPTEMBER 21, 2011

thirty-two
essential #9: meditation...even for restless beginners

....

If that describes you, oh busy friend, I relate. It's taken me years to get to the point where I can sit in regular meditation comfortably for longer than ten minutes. Why? I have a busy mind. Perhaps you do too.

And yet, meditation is one of those things that has been universally known to be great for the body, mind, and soul for more than two thousand years. And for just as long, people have undoubtedly been dealing with distractions.

If you need data to be convinced of the value of meditation, here it is. Study after study have been conducted, and researchers have found that long-term meditators have increased valuable gray matter in their brains. That's even in the frontal cortex, which is associated with working memory, concentration, and executive decision-making, all critical for success in business and life.*

Meanwhile, the brain's fight-or-flight center, the amygdala, shows up in these scans as reduced in size, which could explain why meditators experience so much more calm over time. As noted earlier, this is the center of the brain that produces fear, anxiety, and stress.[†]

In fifty-year-olds, the amount of beneficial gray matter in the brain after regular meditation is similar to that of twenty-five-year-olds, *despite the effects of aging.* Not only that, it only takes eight weeks of meditation for these effects to show up in MRIs. Some participants in these studies meditated forty minutes per day, while others only did so a few times a week for much shorter periods. *The key to beneficial results is to keep the practice going.*[‡]

Overall benefits of meditation include reduced anxiety, improved concentration, healthier impulses, and increased self-awareness.

----

*   Brigid Schulte, "Harvard Neuroscientist: Meditation Not Only Reduces Stress, Here's How It Changes Your Brain," *Washington Post*, May 26, 2015, https://www.washingtonpost.com/news/inspired-life/wp/2015/05/26/harvard-neuroscientist-meditation-not-only-reduces-stress-it-literally-changes-your-brain/?utm_term=.f06080bb380f.

†   Schulte, "Harvard Neuroscientist"; Sue McGreevy, "8 Weeks to a Better Brain," *Harvard Gazette*, January 21, 2011, https://news.harvard.edu/gazette/story/2011/01/eight-weeks-to-a-better-brain/.

‡   Melanie Curtin, "Neuroscience Reveals 50-Year-Olds Can Have Brains of 25-Year-Olds if they Do This One Thing," *Inc.*, October 23, 2018, https://www.inc.com/melanie-curtin/neuroscience-shows-that-50-year-olds-can-have-brains-of-25-year-olds-if-they-do-this.html; McGreevy, "8 Weeks."

Build This into Your Life

Here are a few ideas that will support you in getting into this healthy habit long term, for the good of your brain.

Don't expect too much in the beginning. There is a reason this is called a meditation "practice." It requires a lot of doing over a long time to relax into it. Which is just as it should be.

Start small. Begin with one or two minutes of sitting per day, then ramp up gradually. Ideally, you want to be able to sit for fifteen to twenty or thirty minutes. This will become remarkably easy if you just stick with it.

Trust the process. Eventually, meditation will start to feel good, although you may feel agitated and annoyed at first. Just trust the process, and allow yourself to let go more and more. The longer you do this, the easier it will get. I promise.

Expect insights when you least expect them. Here's how it goes for a lot of us: you begin with big hopes of transcendental highs, but meditation does nothing for you at first. Still, gamely, you soldier on. Then suddenly one day, you get this amazing feeling of serenity, or an intriguing awareness pops in. Or perhaps your body is flushed with happiness or some kind of magical insight. All this is possible with meditation, but only when you truly let go. That requires sticking with it.

Sit comfortably. No, you don't have to sit cross-legged in full lotus position on the cold ground to achieve peace and surrender in meditation. Sitting in a comfortable, straight-backed chair with feet on the floor does the trick just fine. Slouching back into a comfy couch may feel good, but it can also put you to sleep. The goal is to keep your spine fairly straight but not rigidly so. If you feel adventurous, try sitting on the edge of the chair or couch with a cushion or two under your seat so your hips are higher than your knees. Find the best position for you.

Remove distractions. Turn off your phone, close the door, do what you must do to have some moments of peace and quiet. You deserve it. Your meditation time won't be much help if distractions intrude.

Meditate at the start of each day or just before bed. I don't know about you, but I never get to meditation unless it happens first thing each day. I've managed to build in this healthy habit through repetition. Another alternative is to meditate as the last thing you do each day, which can be an effective way to turn off your brain, wind down, and sleep more deeply.

Play a soothing soundtrack. Using one of the apps mentioned previously, such as Insight Timer, can help you stay focused. You create your own soothing background sounds and cues to work with the timer. Mine plays a gentle rainfall, and a subtle gong rings at intervals, letting me know where I am in the meditation. You can also use guided meditations that talk you through the process of slowing down and letting go, if that helps. If you are brand-new to meditation, I recommend this approach.

Explore different types of meditation. If you just can't sit still, there are a variety of seated meditation alternatives online. For instance, consider getting instruction on walking meditation. Or try laughing meditation, which involves...yes...laughing. Or Eastern movement practices like qigong, tai chi, and kundalini, a type of yoga. Yogic breathing can be helpful for clearing the head every day. All this is accessible online.

And all this adds up to increased mindfulness—the art of learning how to settle, still yourself, and be as you move through life, which is at the heart of any meditation practice.

Why am I resisting meditating? Your mind is rushing you and telling you that you have too much else to do. Plus you don't always have to have a huge, long, transformational meditation. A little one can do the same. Listen to your body, what it wants. It wants to relax and connect.

—TEAL'S JOURNAL, OCTOBER 19, 2011

thirty-three
essential #10: feed your brain well

. . . .

Along with resting your brain, great self-care also must include the things that refresh and restore. These are those deeper breaks that really feed our souls. Some might even fit into the same category as Essential #6, Honest-to-God Fun.

The difference is that these elements are important for more than just having fun. They have distinct neurological benefits as well and add balance to our overall mental and emotional conditioning.

Creating a healthy habit around any of these can greatly increase your serenity.

Here are a few good places to turn for nutritious brain food.

Seek mental stimulation. What do you love? Is it a walk in the snow, a visit to the ballet, an afternoon spent knitting by a sunny window? Perhaps a cuddle with your cat, a climb up a desert rock face, or baking a loaf of bread? These are not only soul-healing activities, they provide you with much-needed mental stimulation and relaxation.

Yet many of us exist on a diet of anxiety, deadlines, TV, nagging conversations, and the same old same old. By choosing to return to activities you have been passionate about or have always wanted to try, you send yourself a great big mental hug. And that, in and of itself, can be remarkably healing.

Challenge yourself in new ways. Every day, we move through the world engaging in familiar activities. Yet herein lies the opportunity. Researchers say the key to staving off the eventual mental decline of dementia and Alzheimer's is variety. In other words, dare to do things differently.

If your morning train commute is often spent on work, why not take ten minutes to do a crossword puzzle instead? If you find yourself balking at the idea, ask yourself: Will that ten minutes really make a difference in your overall output if you don't spend it working? Or would the mental stimulation that comes from doing the puzzle be more beneficial?

If your nightly walk with the dog is just around the same old neighborhood, why not drive to a brand-new starting point? And while you're at it, why not listen to a podcast about something you don't usually listen to?

Or if you're the one at home who always cooks dinner, why not learn how to cook with an Instant Pot or master an ethnic cuisine? Or, hell, go read a great book while your beloved cooks dinner instead.

The key is to up your engagement, your challenge level, and your interest. Why not take three minutes per day and do a crossword puzzle or word game delivered by app to your phone? Then gradually keep upping your game as you master each level.

Sing, play, or listen to music. It could be you're a closet singer and some time spent singing in a choir is what's needed now. After all, research indicates that choral singers often synch up breathing and heart rates as they sing together, creating a chorus-wide calming effect.[*] Or, if you have less available free time or you try not to sing in public, try singing in the shower or even hum as you move through your day.

If you don't feel particularly musical, consider this. One of the primary applications of music therapy is for treatment of anxiety, depression, and the physical effects of stress. (And yes, treatment usually includes singing and improvising musically.) If singing isn't your thing, is there a dusty guitar, ukulele, or a piano somewhere in your past? Playing an instrument can have a similar calming effect on the brain.

Neuroscientists have found that listening to music stimulates reward centers in the brain as well, and that can flood us with positive emotions.[†] Plugging into some soothing music may really be what's needed most at day's end.

Exercise. Moderate walks, even for just thirty minutes per day,

---

[*] Claire Groden, "Many Hearts, One Beat: Singing Syncs Up Heart Rates," *Time*, July 10, 2013, http://healthland.time.com/2013/07/10/many-hearts-one-beat-singing-synchs-up-heart-rates/.

[†] Rhonda Freeman, "Music and the Brain's Reward and Bonding Systems," *Psychology Today*, April 28, 2016, https://www.psychologytoday.com/us/blog/neurosagacity/201604/music-and-the-brains-reward-and-bonding-systems.

have been found to stave off mental decline and depression. A team of international researchers has found that as little as one hour of exercise per week truly can shield people from depression.* (See Essential #5.)

Try doodling and coloring. Drexel University researchers have found that aimless doodling releases feelings of pleasure by stimulating your prefrontal cortex.† Not only that, but taking a time-limited doodling break when you are stuck in problem-solving mode can actually produce a creative solution. Doodling has been associated with the fertile default mode the brain enters when doing nothing, which is the place where many creative breakthroughs happen.

Second to this in generating good feelings are drawing and coloring. Adult coloring books, a boon for those who get stopped because they can't draw, have been found to help PTSD, anxiety, and stress. The act of coloring in the lines actually soothes the amygdala, allowing the brain some rest and relaxation. It can also help with increased concentration and organizational skills.‡

If you haven't tried out adult coloring books, Amazon, craft

---

* Maria Cohut, "Just One Hour of Exercise Per Week Could Prevent Depression," *Medical News Today*, October 3, 2017, https://www.medicalnewstoday.com/articles /319607.php.

† Anne Converse Willkomm, "How Drawing and Doodling Boost Creativity," *Professional Studies Blog*, Drexel University Goodwin College of Professional Studies, June 21, 2017, https://drexel.edu/goodwin/professional-studies-blog/overview/2017/June/Doodling/.

‡ Nikki Martinez, "7 Reasons Adult Coloring Books Are Great for Your Mental, Emotional and Intellectual Health," *Huffington Post*, November 24, 2015, https://www.huffpost .com/entry/7-reasons-adult-coloring-books-are-great-for-your-mental-emotional-and -intellectual-health_b_8626136.

stores, and many bookstores carry them along with a variety of colored pencils, gel pens, and the like for filling in pages.

Build This into Your Life

Have a coloring party. Invite some pals over on a weekend afternoon or evening, clear off a table, and have at it. Good music is essential, as are excellent snacks. Make it a potluck if that will increase the likelihood you'll do it, and have everyone come with their favorite coloring book and pens.

Like the idea? Block it off on your calendar now.

While you're at it, close your eyes for a moment and take three deep, slow breaths. Then tune in to yourself quietly for a moment. Ask your brain what kind of stimulation it would like from you at the moment.

When you're ready, open your eyes, and feed that request. Or block out a bit of time on your calendar to make it happen. Reminder: This doesn't have to be a big deal. Short and easy will do the trick. And no request is too mundane. They're all not only good ideas, they also are important.

When you worry, bad flow begins. When you put out good energy, it leads to good flow.

—TEAL'S JOURNAL, SEPTEMBER 12, 2011

part three

working self-care into your life

thirty-four
folding self-care
habits into your day

. . . .

So how do you take this abundance of self-care ideas and work at least some of them into your extremely busy life? The answer is simple—you must be willing to make some changes. By now, you've had a chance to see what you can add and what you can let go of.

But in the end, all it really takes is willingness. So...are you willing?

Now you also understand that this process is best done with support, whether that's a good friend, an action buddy, or some professional helpers. A live support group or possibly even our Facebook group might also be a boon to you. Whatever you choose, do not attempt to make these changes alone. Get help where needed, for that may make all the difference.

Reminder: I am asking you to get out of your comfort zone and put yourself first. If that brings up feelings of uncertainty or anxiety, please do get a buddy, a group, or some kind of support to bolster you. And keep the faith! This process will get seriously comfortable very quickly. You just have to get over the hump and get on with it.

Secondly, keep your eye on the prize. Remember that even if some of these actions seem challenging at first, they are going to lead you back to balance. And *nothing* feels better than that!

Still, if you know yourself to be a procrastinator or avoider when it comes to things that are good for you or if you still think you're just too busy for self-care, read on. This part is for you.

The most important thing is to build automatic self-care habits into your routine.

You can have all the good intentions in the world, but habits are what actually change your behavior long term. In his excellent book, *The Power of Habit*, Charles Duhigg explains how. A well-rewarded habit honors the wiring of our brains, which makes them remarkably effective.

As Duhigg explains, habits begin with a cue and conclude with a reward. This is true for both negative and beneficial habits. Think about it. If you're a nail-biter, your cue is low-level anxiety, your habit is a good nail chew, and your reward is a release of tension and a greater sense of ease.

Now what if that process got applied to, say, exercise?

To set up the healthy exercise habit, first establish a cue that rings the exercise bell. For me, it's that tired feeling at the end of the afternoon that means I've done enough work at my desk. Another cue for me is looking at the clock and seeing it's almost 4:00 p.m. Then comes a good walk or a workout at the gym, followed by the reward of an endorphin rush and my very satisfying swipe of my accountability app, signaling that I got the job done.

At this point, this habit is so ingrained, I actually miss exercise when it doesn't happen. That is the power of a good, healthy habit.

What will your own reward be for, say, working out? Will that be your own endorphin high? Or the sauna and shower that follows? Or sitting down to play with your child when you get home?

Note: May I just say that, tempting as it is, a cookie is not a productive reward. At least not if your goal is abundant energy. (Trust me on this. I made that mistake. And ten pounds later, I finally decided it was a bad idea.) Instead, look for the payoffs that best serve your long-term goal of true self-care.

I say the best habit rewards are free and that they simply emerge from your routine with ease. You'll know your cue when you see it, and you'll know your reward as well.

Here's another thing I love about habits: you don't have to think about them. And if you stack habits in different time zones, like first thing in the morning, you can pack in all kinds of good stuff. Begin with the ones you resist the most. For me, that's meditation.

My cue for meditation is waking up and reaching for my phone to read my news app. I naturally see my meditation timer, so the cue registers. I allow myself a leisurely stroll through the daily news headlines, then I head out to the same spot every morning in my living room to meditate. When the bell goes off signaling I've completed my meditation, I'm left with a relaxed, happy feeling of peace, which is my reward. It only takes fifteen minutes, and already my day is going well.

This is followed by drinking water, taking supplements, doing stretches, making a gratitude list, and a few other self-care essentials. By then, half an hour has gone by, and I'm feeling fired up, inspired, and ready for the day.

My list of morning self-care habits will undoubtedly be different from yours. The key is to craft that list so you get just what you need and to experiment until you get it right. It took me a year to realize I didn't have to meditate for thirty minutes every day. For me, fifteen does the trick.

Either way, by filling that first forty-five minutes of the day with quick and easy self-care habits, I've already done something amazing for myself, so I am far more prepared for whatever life throws at me. Also helpful is doing this early, before others wake up and potentially throw you off your game.

I now understand why my mother used to get up and make coffee a full two hours before her four kids had to leave for school. She was getting in her me time.

If you're not a morning person and/or your morning is mainly occupied with getting children off to school, there is still hope. Save some time in the middle or end of your workday or when the house is quiet before bed. Find that time when you can just do your own thing, undisturbed, for a little while.

Habits are also helpful when it comes to, say, eating a healthier diet. A nutritionist once advised me to eat a cereal-bowl-sized portion of steamed veggies each day as well as a salad of the same size. Which I do nearly every day. Habit = veggies. Done.

I also throw some flaxseed oil on that salad every day, as recommended to keep one's digestion humming along, which brings up the idea of combining healthy habits.* Look for places where the habits you want to build can intersect. Another good combo is listening to a podcast while exercising. This is helpful for catching up on professional content you might not ordinarily get to or, in the self-care vein, something on a subject you've been longing to explore.

If you find habits are not working for you, consider the mini habit. These are reserved for those healthy habits you absolutely cannot make yourself do. The creator of the mini habit, Stephen Guise, challenged himself one day to do one push-up. That's all. Just one. Which he did easily...and then naturally followed with ten more.[†]

The mental trick of mini habits gets us over the hump of avoiding something because it appears to be too large and difficult. Try breaking off a tiny self-care task you keep avoiding—five minutes of exercise or eating one bite of salad. Then see where that leads you.

- - - - - - - - - - - - - - - - - -

[*]   Madeline R. Vann, "How Flaxseed Benefits Digestion," Everyday Health, July 26, 2010, https://www.everydayhealth.com/digestive-health/how-flaxseed-benefits-digestion .aspx; Rachael Link, "6 Benefits of Flaxseed Oil—Plus How to Use It," Healthline, September 29, 2017, https://www.healthline.com/nutrition/flaxseed-oil-benefits #section4.

[†]   Stephen Guise, *Mini Habits: Smaller Habits, Bigger Results* (self-pub., 2013), 12–13.

Creating Your Ideal Self-Care Schedule

The very best way to create greater self-care in your life and build in these much-desired habits is to schedule it. If this seems impossible in your overcrowded day, I want to ask you something.

Have you locked yourself into a lack of self-care by not making any kind of room for it on your schedule? Pull out your calendar right now, and take a look. The results may surprise you.

Since most of us extremely busy women are schedule-oriented, it stands to reason that this is where we should begin.

But here's the good news: you can begin to create a brand-new life based on what you truly want and need. Right here and right now. All it takes is willingness and a bit of planning.

Do the exercises that follow. Then take the self-care activities you've selected on the Three Self-Care Actions to Begin Now list on page 265 and put them into your calendar. Put them on automatic repeat in your calendar if you want to continue to do them regularly.

Then don't give in to any temptation to blow them off when the time arrives.

Instead, step out of the habitual comfort zone of overwork, and actually do the self-care activity instead. Make sure you add at least one activity to your calendar for every day of the week. Ideally, add more. Or create a self-care zone, as described earlier, in which you can batch several self-care habits.

As far as online scheduling tools go, I work with Google Calendar, which makes functions like auto repeat easy. (There are many other online options as well, such as iCal.) I also like to use Google

Calendar's separate color-coded calendars, so I can see at a glance how the balance is between work, self-care, and the rest of my life.

If you look at your calendar and have no idea where you're going to squeeze in a bit of me time, take a second look. Do you really have to do every single task booked on your calendar? Is there some way you can outsource some of it or simply take certain responsibilities off your to-do list? Is it possible to get some help?

Reminder: this may be your chance to let go of the need for perfection and overdelivery.

The ability to let go of tasks and obligations is what separates the women from the girls, for you and I both know some things can always be delegated. You really can slice and dice your time any way you want. In the end, the choice is always yours.

By the same token, if your schedule is erratic and changes from day to day, make a commitment to adding one self-care task per day or even every other day. If you tend to make promises to yourself and then forget or avoid them, make that promise with your buddy. And put it on your calendar.

If you're still in avoidance mode about self-care scheduling, ask yourself if you are intentionally vague on this for a reason. If so, it could be this thinking is just an old habit that no longer serves you.

Bottom line: do what you can to fit some self-care actions into each day. If they use up no more than fifteen minutes, call it good. For now. And understand that Rome wasn't built in a day, so your own self-care habits may take some time to expand and develop.

Once you really get on the self-care train and you begin to experience true self-love and self-support, you're going to want more. I promise you. Play with your schedule over time to try to find the perfect self-care balance for you. And don't be afraid to add more and more self-care as you realize how fantastic it makes you feel.

Do you have enough exercise, playtime with your children, or connection time with your spouse or friends? Do you have enough me time? Do you go to sleep at night feeling sleepy and satisfied or flattened by the steamroller of your life? If it's the latter, then more self-care needs to be scheduled in.

When the system breaks down, which it probably will, it's important to determine why. Check in and find out what happened. Did you give up on yourself briefly, and if so, why? Is there someone or something you're making more important than yourself?

This is really a good opportunity to learn more about your own thinking.

In the end, friends, bear in mind that all this is a great big experiment. Our only job in life is to try, fail, try, succeed, try, tweak, and try again until we either succeed or we get tired of that particular experiment.

In the meantime, begin the delicious task of actively allowing more self-care into your life.

I promise you won't regret it.

It is time to start delegating and being in your power. Step up and be a leader of love!

—TEAL'S JOURNAL, SEPTEMBER 17, 2011

..... T W E N T Y M I N U T E S .....

Design Your Perfect Day

Write down a list of people, places, and things that all would be part of your perfect day at home and at work. Do not let reason interfere with what your soul and your imagination dish up.

My Perfect Day at Work

My Perfect Day at Home

Is there anything here you can add to your life right now? If so, put it on the schedule now.

thirty-five
how to stay committed to your own self-care

. . . .

Life happens.

That's why this chapter covers what to do when you find yourself repeatedly blowing off your self-care activities. Or you find yourself wanting to revert back to old, less-than-healthy behaviors. Or when you just can't get yourself to set some much-needed boundaries with someone.

As ever, it's time to ask yourself a few questions. First of all, what's going on at this exact moment? The twelve-step philosophy of the HALT principle may apply here. Are you avoiding the good stuff because you're hungry, angry, lonely, or tired?

Or is there some bigger issue at hand? Perhaps you're fighting the flu, or you just had a fight with your spouse, or your request for a raise was denied.

Life, as I said earlier, can get gnarly sometimes. However, that's okay. You can always pick yourself up and get back on track—no harm, no foul. Or you can blow off the entire notion of self-care. The path is entirely up to you.

But if you do want to stay engaged with these ideas, another question must be asked. What do you need right now?

Really stop and find out. Close your eyes. Breathe. Check in with yourself. Because whether or not you actually do build self-care into your life, you now understand the immense power of listening to your body.

So what is she asking for? And how can you provide it?

It may be that your body and soul are asking you to build in a little slack to go along with all the good intentions. Go ahead and allow yourself to have that donut once in a while in order to stay committed to the diet. And that's just fine. You have to figure out what works for you.

One of the dangers of a book like this—or any personal development program—is that you use it to bludgeon yourself with good intentions. Please do not vow that you will never miss a workout, eat sugar, or stay up late for the rest of your life.

Instead, please be kind to yourself and gradually phase in the ideas here that appeal to you. And feel free to blow off the rest.

Remember that you, too, are a work in progress, just like the rest of us. And the only voice really worth listening to is your own.

My hope is that this book will help you stay tuned in to you and your precious inner voice and that it will guide you back to peace, ease, and an abundant, joyful life. For that is the ultimate gift of self-care.

Learn to love every moment.
Every moment is beautiful.
Every moment is a lesson.

—TEAL'S JOURNAL, JULY 11, 2011

Great Self-Care Actions

Need ideas for self-care? I started the list for you, to help the self-care juices flow. Add as many as you can. Use this list to build your new self-care routine.

1. Meditation
2. Yoga
3. A healthy diet (low or no sugar, fewer carbs, lots of vegetables, adequate protein)
4. A little excellent, high-quality dark chocolate now and then
5. Relaxed, unproductive time with a child
6. Choosing a healthy smoothie instead of a dessert or junk food
7. Hiking, biking, or walking in nature alone or with a friend
8. Workouts with support
9. Reading really good books, maybe visiting a library and bringing home the max number allowed
10. Lounging around on the couch for no reason
11. Doing a puzzle
12. Visiting a local museum or gallery you've been wanting to get to
13. Sleeping in
14. Dancing
15. Going out to a good movie
16. Spending regular time with your love or your dear friends just hanging out
17. Playing games with the people you love
18. Walking the dog with someone you care about

19. Cooking a great meal for yourself and/or others

20. Regularly attending a church, temple, mosque, sangha, or meditation center

21. Singing (even in the shower)

22. Going out dancing or taking dancing lessons

23. Booking regular vacations, even if they are staycations

24. Browsing or window-shopping in an interesting place

25. Taking yourself out for coffee and leaving your phone at home

26. Calling or meeting a dear friend for coffee

27. Calling Mom, Dad, or your kids just to say hi

28. Signing up for any kind of race, walkathon, etc., and training for it

29. Spending time making your bucket list

30. Journaling on the questions in the back of this book

31. Putting on some earbuds or headphones and listening to beautiful music

32. Volunteering somewhere that really feeds your soul

33. Setting an effective limit where it's overdue

34. Going to the theater

35. Gardening and growing things

36. _____

37. _____

38. _____

39. _____

40. _____

41. _____

42. _____

43. ....
44. ....
45. ....
46. ....
47. ....
48. ....
49. ....
50. ....

····· FIVE MINUTES ·····

Three Self-Care Actions to Begin Right Now

Pick three things from the list in the previous exercise. Which ones feel most urgent or desirable to you? Write them below. Ideally, make two of them important self-care items and one of them something that's just plain fun.

....

....

....

....

....

Great! Now add them to your schedule.

Design Your Perfect Self-Care Plan

Keep a loose, evolving list of self-care items here that you'd like to build into your schedule. Feel free to return to this list again and again, developing it as you go. As you write down self-care actions, also note when you might fit them in. Consult with this list when building your self-care schedule and keeping your self-care log.

Action	When

····· FIVE MINUTES ·····

The Advantages of Keeping a Self-Care Log

Here's your chance to get clear on how much self-care you actually include in your life. At the end of the day, just write in whatever your self-care action is. Then rate your overall well-being and happiness at the end of the day on a scale of 1 to 10.

You'll discover what lights you up. But you'll also get to track exactly how much time you give to self-care and how much you actually need to operate at your best.

Note: In rating each activity, 1 is abject misery, while a 10 is peaceful, joyful, and very happy indeed!

For best results, keep this log regularly for at least two months. Turn to page 290 for a full self-care log sheet.

Example

Action #1	Action #2	Action #3	Action #4	Happiness Score
Meditate	Walk in woods	Bath	Fun reading	8.5

thirty-six
self-care on
your phone

....

Your phone is more than just a conveyer of unread texts and a screen that sucks up your attention. It's also a clever little self-care machine. An entire host of self-care apps can be downloaded to support all areas of your life.

You can track everything from how soundly you sleep to the carb composition of your food, how much water you drink, and how much fun you're having in life. An entire host of meditation apps support you to stick with that critical piece of your self-care. Accountability apps keep you on track with fitness and wellness goals of all types as well.

To keep the list as current as possible, I made a list of my favorite apps in a free document you can download from my website.

May it serve you well!

A List of My Favorite Self-Care Apps

For a current collection of self-care apps that I've found useful, which include everything from accountability apps to sleep enhancement and meditation apps, please see my most recent list.

To get you started, here are my four most critical self-care apps I've found useful nearly every day.

Health (on iOS) or Fit (on Android)

It doesn't matter when you walk, only that you do. And these apps will track not only how many steps you've taken, but how many flights you've climbed, throughout the day. You don't even have to set up these apps—they're busy recording your physical activity all the time. They both can track other areas of your personal health as well.

Spotify

This is a paid music, podcast, and audio streaming service I use for yoga nidra meditations nearly every morning. I find myself using their Daily Mix feature for soothing background music while I work. A free version is also available.

WW

If you want to get rid of persistent extra pounds, WW will get you there for a low monthly fee. The Weight Watchers SmartPoints system helps you evaluate everything you eat and your portion sizes. Not only that, a barcode scanner will tell you the SmartPoints value before you even add it to your grocery cart. More than four thousand healthy recipes are another included feature.

Insight Timer

If you want to keep a meditation practice going, but it's gotten stale, old, or hard to do, make it fun! Insight Timer has more than twenty thousand free guided visualizations and meditations to choose from. You can also create a lovely timer of chimes to keep your own silent meditations on track.

Visit suzannefalter.com/self-care-apps/ for more and up-to-date apps I love.

thirty-seven
more fun deciding how to live

. . . .

By now, I hope you have gotten the picture that your self-care is really like a gorgeous puzzle with which you get to endlessly tinker. Remember, the answers are all there, tucked into your heart and soul, waiting to be discovered.

You are not meant to live a life of quiet (or even loud) drudgery any more than you are meant to suffer to be significant. Instead, I'd like to suggest a life of ease and flow, driven by that which lights you up.

This is why self-care ultimately becomes about slowing down to the speed of life, as my friend Jon puts it. It's also about checking in with your soul and learning what makes you tick. That's why we will end this book with workbook pages of great questions to consider with a cup of tea, a pen, and some paper.

Explore these lists and questions by writing them out in a

notebook or typing them into a doc. Use the remaining pages in this book to journal on the following questions.

Want to take your self-care even further? You can find a treasure trove of additional checklists, worksheets, and more on my website's free resource center, at suzannefalter.com/freeresources.

My *Self-Care for Extremely Busy Women* podcast also has interviews nearly every week with self-care experts of all kinds, plus soothing meditations and essays.

Remember you've got gold in there. You simply have to listen to your body, your heart, and your soul to know exactly how to take extraordinary care of yourself.

Thank you for caring enough about yourself to dive into your own self-care. Think of it as your own precious gift to the world.

You are the light of being.
Stay with that and your
sun will shine bright.

—TEAL'S JOURNAL, AUGUST 12, 2011

My Bucket List of Things to Do Before I Die

Five Things I'd Love to Add to My Life

People I've Been Meaning to Call
and What I Would Tell Them

What I Believe I'm Still Capable of Doing

What Holds Me Back from
Living My True Potential

Regrets I Have and What I Learned from Them

Ten Important Things I Learned from Love

Twenty Things I'm Grateful for Right Now

(This one is especially useful if you're in a blue mood.)

Five Ways I Could Improve My Life Right Now

Thoughts That Hold Me Back

Some Ideas That Fire Me Up

Things I'd Do If I Had Ten Times More Courage

Reasons I've Avoided Self-Care

Self-Care Actions I'd Love to Try

My Core Values and the Things I Care About

People I Admire and Why

You have the opportunity
to shine so brightly.
Just honor your body and
stay true to yourself.
You are a goddess.

—TEAL'S JOURNAL, AUGUST 9, 2011

your self-care log

	ACTION #1	ACTION #2
monday		
tuesday		
wednesday		
thursday		
friday		
saturday		
sunday		

ACTION #3	ACTION #4	Happiness Score

	ACTION #1	ACTION #2
monday		
tuesday		
wednesday		
thursday		
friday		
saturday		
sunday		

ACTION #3

ACTION #4

Happiness
Score

acknowledgments

A book is always the sum of many parts, so I extend a great big thanks in many directions. Thank you to Dr. Rima Goldman; Dr. Karen Kartch; Robert Weinberg, PhD; Dale Marie Golden; and Gudren Zomerland for all the great ideas and information.

I also wish to thank those who encouraged this project from the beginning: Annelise Robey; Anna Michels; the Sourcebooks team; and my go-to business and career advisors, Laila, Rachael, Kim, and Robert.

Also, I received support from the many voices of the Self-Care Group for Extremely Busy Women on Facebook and my excellent assistant, Danielle Acee Hartman. Thank you as well to my wife, Rachel Ginsburg, for her loving support of this project.

Finally, I am grateful for the life and sparkling presence of my daughter, Teal Barns, whose wise insights grace many of these pages. I am proud to share her legacy with you.

about the author

Suzanne Falter is an author, speaker, blogger, and podcaster who has published both fiction and nonfiction, as well as essays. She also speaks about self-care, organ donation, and the transformational healing of crisis, especially in her own life after the death of her daughter, Teal. Her nonfiction books include *How Much Joy Can You Stand?, The Joy of Letting Go,* and *Surrendering to Joy.*

Suzanne's essays have appeared in *O Magazine,* the *New York Times, Elephant Journal, Tiny Buddha,* and *Thrive Global,* among others. Her fiction titles include the Oaktown Girls series of lesbian romances and the romantic suspense series Transformed. Suzanne is also the host of the podcast *Self-Care for Extremely Busy Women.* Her nonfiction work, blog, podcasts, and her online course, Self-Care for Extremely Busy Women, can be found at suzannefalter.com and on Facebook, Twitter, Instagram, YouTube, and Pinterest. She lives with her wife in the San Francisco Bay Area.